The Nature of Self

The Nature of Self

An ontology

Jeffrey B. Holl

I.C.H.Publishing Inc.

Produced in affiliation with the Freedom of Expression component of the Canadian *Charter of Rights and Freedoms*, **Canadian Heritage** directive (see *fundamental freedoms* section (2b)).

First edition
Created, Edited and Typeset in Canada
I.C.H. Publishing, Wpg., MB.
Email: godfreyb.holl@outlook.com

Library and Archives Canada
ISBN 978-1-7752848-6-4

Cover Design by Art Self

Jeffrey B. Holl 1970-

The Nature of Self.
Copyright./dedication/contents/preface/chapter 1/chapter 2/
chapter 3/chapter 4/notes/afterword/notes/index/
acknowledgments

10987654321

For the one that listens and always hears, the one that speaks and always conveys, the one that exists and is ever real—the universal soul that radiates divinity but is ever human, the transformative being that is of the natural world.

Contents

Preface

The natural self is the self of nature or the nature-self. It is the objectivation of the Self as itself and of itself, transformed by and through the ordination of the experience of nature as both societal and transcendental. Insofar as it is transcendental it is also natural, and only insofar as it is natural is it transcendental. Being becomes of this through the reality of its own transformation from a transcendental horizon to the existence of the Self upon a natural horizon that is within conception—the being of transcendental nature. It is thus that we become of both the nature to our own transformation, and the transformation of the nature within ourselves into beings that are intentional toward the horizon of our transmissible existentiality, as whole beings within the capacitation of the reality of content that is represented to the mind as the genuine context wherethrough we realize the form of our own transmutability and holistic enterprise. We are both the actuality of the latter, while the formalization of the transitional context wherethrough the content of what is truthful to existence is self-same to the form by which the experience of the Self as subject is within a propositional conception that is immediate and concrete, but also negative and abstract. We are the positivity of the abstraction and the negativity of the concrete, the negativity of the abstraction and the positivity in concretion. Through the genus of a universality that is the reality of the age in which we still live, and the completion of the age in the reality of the genesis of our own particularity—as those seeking the absolution of the measure by which all universal concerns are either adopted or dismissed, under the precondition that the spiritual transformation by which all such conclusions are to become the soul of humanity—we have yet to instantiate a vertical position that is both shaped by nature governing laws just as it is the transcendental positions from which the symbolic dimensions to thought may become realizations to the moment of our arrival within the truth of the becoming of our own universal conceptions of a nature, that is not driven by consumptive behaviour—but rather conceived as a universality that is within the conception of our positions as the realities in which we all posit truth as we understand it, reality as we perceive it. The manner through which the explorations of our behaviours within a spiritual awakening is the reality of our age is still within conception, upon the horizon of the actuality where we conceive ourselves as those within a purposive meaning that constitutes the being of the understanding of ourselves as either products of nature, or products of history. That we are both is the process wherethrough the realization of our governing purposes underlies the sole reason for this existence to be posited as both natural and transcendental. The purpose of our times is to become of this actuality, to realize through the spiritual rendering a casting upon the world of the nature-self as a reality to humanity—that we are and have always been in a world of nature—beings driven within limitation, apathetic toward our passions, consumptive in pleasure, reductive in pain, productive in purpose or consumptive to meaning—beings that are imaginary or real, symbolic or fictitious. As existences that are objective and immediate in the Self, life's meaning is within the context of the idea of Self as it is in its most authentic form—the content which composes transcendental subjectivity, rendering both the structure of belief, just as it does the purpose that makes us complete in the wholeness of our own transcendental nature. We are both form and substance, existence and essence. The form of this existence lies within the reason that we are determinative to our ownership of purpose, and the purposiveness of what we determine to hold as the property of our natural Self. We yearn and struggle to assume a direction in the world that reproduces the awareness of the universality of our means, and the entirety of our experience of ourselves as total in Being. Such is the modality of the intentions that are self-generating by the spiritual awakening that is posited by the mind, once we have come to realize the consummation of the drives delivering us from our demons, upon a landscape of actual correspondence with the beauty of change and the changes that enlighten human consciousness into itself and of itself. The promise of humanity rests in the moment where we become actual to ourselves, realizing the faculty of representation as one that presents us with the reality that we have always sought and were unwilling to face— and the healing must begin from within ourselves, as ourselves, for the amelioration of the histories from which the pain of this life had sprung. We must begin to see the meaning of our time in the here and now of the purposed existence that we wish to call our own.

The Nature of Self

Chapter 1

I consider as belonging to the essence of a thing that, which being given, is necessarily given also, and, which being removed, the thing is necessarily removed also; in other words, that without which the thing, and which itself without the thing, can neither be conceived nor be removed. —Spinoza

§1.1 *Being as pure concept of the Self, and the nature of experience.*

To establish what in fact *is* a pure concept of the Self, it will become necessary to reflect upon what a *self* is. For by conception alone we do not encounter the notion of ourselves being in possession of a self and the presupposition that the latter constitutes the nature of being or the experiences that accommodate the acknowledgement that we are conscious of ourselves, such that we recognize within us the attributes that are particular to our own natures. With this, it is that the conception of the self is to be considered the conception of our natures, as we reflect from the sources of the substances that constitute human undertaking upon this planet and provide the environment by which all concepts of the self are posited from the universal context in which the notions of self were first conceived as total throughout the process of identification.[1] It is as such that *Being* elicits this conception and conjoins to primordial humans in such a way as to open an ontological context such that the experience of self is both conception as it is nature—and thereto the nature of experience as the very embodiment of the consciousness from where the generative components of the psyche could be conceived as natural *to* conception.   Such that the former is something that necessarily posits an awareness of what exists, what constitutes experience is always in question.

From the genesis of the early stages of our involvement with the conception of the self from its origination in and through Being, we encountered self-realization as an adjunct to the conception of self as being nothing proprietary or observed, but both proprietary and observed through experience.[2] The conception of the self is also accommodated by an ordination of reason that is conceptually facilitated by *being* as the very conception of existence—which renders the notion of Self even more observational as an entity that has actual possession of an inheritance of experience—as though the pre-conception of Being satisfactorily suffices in making allowances for the experiences themselves to be delivered as realities that are neither true nor false, but only exist as propositions to what is fact and what is fiction. Being necessitates the experience of the Self as an abstraction, just as it does the prepossession of the nature of experience that is posited by the mind rather than conceived. The self is in fact, precisely as it is conceived from its originary encounter with Being, providing the necessary coordinates for all that is, from the prepossession of the Being of nature as pure concept of the Self, and the nature of the experiences that are particular to the former as entrances into the natural environment where the experiences that establish the necessary context for self-identification become a part of perceptual reality of horizons upon which all such activities constitute the sustainability of being and the conception of self and its natural encumbrances.

Humanity is as such Being with a Self as its concept, and nature the experience of the former with the latter as it stands in relation to other like and unlike existences that are part of the same natural environment in which beings and selves are apportioned to two separated realities: the reality of the *subject,* and the reality of the *object.*[3] Such as it is, Being as Self, constitutes the conception of the latter as pure to the experiences that are universal, and impure in relation to the experiences of the former that are particular to the universal self-concept. The nature of universality is one that is particular to every self-concept, but the nature of its experiences nullifies the universality of the Self and renders the conception out of reach of the purity of its origination in the universality of nature. By these means alone, the self-concept[4] is, as such, only a means by which Being realizes its purpose and becomes as is necessary in order to provide for the primordial essence that accompanies the experience of Being as it is from its first stage as an object to the Self, while becoming subjective through its first natural experiences with the environmental conditions as they exist *a priori*. Such as the natural environs in which the self is awakened to the purposes that are motivations or biological necessities to the very conception of Self, they become post-cognitive drives which propel the conceptions of self to the point where the experiences that are conferred upon a Self become perceptions to *existence in-itself*. Such as it is, existence proper is simply the natural experience of Being in relation to the self-concept and the natural environment where the aforementioned are situated. Now this environment, posited as natural, *is* only so insofar as the coordinates of the self-concept are *intersubjectively* entwined, and *interobjectively* activated. Beings as such may be both natural and unnatural, selves and not-selves—existences that are inventions of the natural world that has bestowed upon primordial humanity something that has become of the conflicts between natural existences and the experiences here to be thought of as natural cognitive biases that are pre-reflexive to self-concepts and the conditions opposed to the naturalization of Being as self-concept, and its universality as conditioned by the teleological origins that had posited Being as existence, and mind as the natural experience of the self-concept that is abstracted from its conceptual origination in the biosphere.

The question of nature providing Being with essence has been thought out by philosophers from Spinoza to Hegel, and it is here that we come to the conclusion that for the furtherance of the discipline, the time has come to acknowledge our place in the cosmos as planetary and provisionally awakened by the teleological connection to the latter as the very source of this which binds us to the very conception of ourselves, as Beings that have become aware of the naturalistic possibilities of experience having taken root within the environment that had conditioned the responses to the substance governing natural law. It is with this, that the Being of ourselves is wed to the conception of Self that has occurred from the precognitive conditionality of the positional stance from where a self might be conditioned by natural causes and awareness of the universality of nature and the telos of the coordinates from where the self-concept is posited as an *actual existent of natural experience*.[5]   Where the self is of its own generative conceptualization, it is also that Being is the Self as it exists in relation to its counterposition in the existences of nature as they exist in their positive state of self-actualization.

But what is counter to the Self—and can be actual in a naturalized environment of primordial *humanicization*[6]—is actual to the self as a concept that is expunged from the coordinates from where actualities are intelligible existences that are outside of reason as the driving force of actuality and counter to the intuitive conceptions of self. For this reason, the self is alone from the moment its counterpositional object is instantiated as a judgment seeking propositional influence. Yet, upon this threshold it is not that we are even aware of the latter, as though the concept of self necessarily resides in the conception of its natural experience as constitutive of the self-concept, and never this which is unnatural to the conditions presupposed by nature as the very context whereby nature remains universal to the self-concept—thereby undermining the *telos* by which undulations to the understanding would become particularizations rather than truths, posited by the natural experience of the horizons from which abstractions of the naturalized self-concept are posited universally in accordance with the natural laws that determine Being as the essence of primordial humanity.

§1.2 *Being representation as an empirical object of the understanding.*
Empirical objects are here to be contemplated as objects of the natural world i.e., the phenomena causally produced by the elements of nature and the environment of substances that create the necessary conditions for the experience of these phenomena as objects of the understanding.[7] As such, they are necessarily posited in relations that are conditional to the understanding, yet the natural objects in consideration are never within justification objects to rational discourse—they are rather phantoms of the mind reproducing community relations that are identifiable as these which are not considerate of the laws of reason that must accompany them. However, as the universal human essence is a mediating power to the understanding, the Self undergoes its particularization into a state of reified

universal singularity—conjoined only to the substance of relations that are posited by the representative Self as a Being that is formed through its own contemplative acts of reification. But as it stands, we know not what the concept of reification entails, as we are only in the beginning of a dialectic that must inevitably ensue. Aye, we know not yet what is in its effects the concept of dialectic e're the discourse at hand enters a disposition that is less than admirable to the currency of the investitures at hand. We do not deny what is at hand given the empirical understanding as it relates to the thoughts of Locke or Hume—where objects are these that are received from nature but possess no metaphysical accompaniment, such as would be far from me to deny is here based upon autosuggestion more than it is upon the previous claims of a finality to the metaphysical project through its most generational presence in physics—concerning the laws which govern conceptions of phenomena as real to the understanding and posited as identifiable to a reality that is particular to the prepossession of a Self *as* objective. The question remains, if we first possess an awareness of the object as the natural entitlement to Being, is it not then true that the object is the object of *itself,* the Self as object to itself and for its representational performance within the universality that had first posited the object as its necessary particularization into a subject with givens? Such as it stands, this object is not yet the Self, but stands in relation to the Self as it is in its natural environment and must now become an object *for* the Self and the very representation by which the self becomes universal in representation as a Self that is *Being.* Such that the latter is in question of Self as *object* it is not only an object to the self but also an object of the self—the self of existence that is posited and may be abstracted or depart locus of judgment for other loci—consigning upon the Self a subjective particularization that is relative to the conditions of the very universality that had first posited an object for the self. As such this object is the empirical object of the understanding as conditioned by nature, and posits the necessary conditional acts of the self in subsequent pursuit of the necessary activity preemptive of the coordinates of its contingent articulation—such that the presuppositions to being are never these driven by the thing-in-itself alone, but are actualities posited by an acting self that is willful in presentation and representation as an object of knowledge to the universal understanding. The representations of Self are never contingently opposed, but actively closed in operations that are contiguous to the particularizations of the Self as it is conditioned in retreat from its opposition from the telos of nature. This struggle continues through the representational factions accompanying the self as a self of nature that stands in relation to other selves that are opponents of the necessary particularization posited by contingency—forming the space where the purposiveness of the Self stands only in relation to its universal instauration as a necessary self of nature that is absolute to the precognitive biases that will necessarily oppose the natural phenomena that inheres of the subject as itself. These correspond and intersect with the absolutes of nature through science in a transformation of the elements of nature, into actual representations understood as realities in contemplation. The primordial understanding, if you will, is conditioned by something that is universal to nature and to humanity is abstracted *a priori* by human nature and posited as universal to the Self and its representative potentiality.

But for Being to represent something through nature—the objects of the elements such as they are phenomena—happens through the contingent articulation of what is *particular* to the understanding of another self. Such as it is, this posits an act of judgment that is universal to the understanding of the Self that has already reflexively objectified its own relational status. Given that nature is the *telos* of all operative actualities that constitute the self-concept *as* representation, we now may come to understand how we are perceived at the *societal* level. As this is altogether another dimension to the human understanding, I propose that the essential horizon of truth be posited as one that is proprietary to the Being of nature, and that the former merely casts its shadow of belonging in order to obscure the coordinates of the truth from their natural position upon the locus of judgment. Such that we must know ourselves, we must also realize the true potential of our natures and understand the environmental context in which they occur as realities to Being. With this as representation, the self is relative only to its own particularization within a knowing universal genus of existence—an actuality that is posited by the mind, toward the horizon of its own reflexive understanding. Things as such are transitional to the context wherethrough Beings are transformed as actualities and become of the forms that accompany their instantiation as complexions of a natural environmental whole. By these extraordinary means, the world possesses many creatures of *global* complexity in its wilderness—for every species that becomes extinct, there are most certainly new ones coming into existence through the natural evolutionary dynamic reducible only to its most favoured—accomplished of the logically supranatural Beings that have been emerging upon this planet—once thought to have merely been suffering from an appropriation of their innermost truthful selves, while reforming the conception of what is natural to human excrescence. To depart the animal kingdom with a keen sense of judgment, upon the heels of one's most fruitful judgmental stance affordable, the likelihood that we will come to realize the full potential of humanity as an existence that is unmediated by particularizations from the *telos* of the societal context where they had become designators as reified from a normativity structured by its positionality transitional from the originary context where it had achieved its form, one must contemplate the purposive meaning identifiable within the conception of humanity as something that is in prepossession of a normative bias that has been structured by contemplative acts, alone in pursuit of societal norms that have become unnatural to the very context wherethrough the realities of the telos of nature would become activated as structural to human understanding—uncompromised by a universality that had ordered genus from its transformational proximation in the psyche as a content-bearing form that had achieved its instauration as an objective representation that had not been expressed throughout a division between the Self and its objective counterposition—but rather was the very complexion by which substance were reified as proximal to the understanding, as it conjoins with the verisimilitude of the essence that had posited the mediation of the universal context where it had been generated by the *telos* of nature.[8] The latter is, in effect, consumed by a Self as it realizes the positional contextualization of its ordinance within the naturalization of itself as a reified object that must become transformative of its own *onto-teleological* enterprise. Such that this bespeaks of its elegance with an appropriation of Kant, is never to become conditional to the reification positional to the representational locus from which the coordinates of judgment are to become exclusive to the ordination of what composes the empiricism at stake in our present discourse. For what is resisting the very consumption of its own rubric, is the designation of the object as something composed of the Self *a priori*. In effect, it is this that is in question, or whether, to wit, one might propose that a Self is without limitation—such that the world is every-thing, and substance a universality of coordinates accompanying Being unto the horizon of a wilderness that might only be transformed through the universality of a quite proprietary ordination of unsubstantiated, localized claims that condone the order of nature as something provisional to those with social status and a vitality of glad handing, predicated upon the conception of humanity as something other than its reflexive self-conception—the nature of *Being* as the notion of what has become representational to the human understanding. Insofar as reasoned thoughts may be representative to human understanding, so are the spoken words that accompany them. It is in this way the ordination of Being becomes of its contingent articulation into the objectification of the Self as a knowing subject. The acts of the Self as an inward Being are the reifications of the ontological field of perception.

§1.3 *transcendental objective signification, the historical cultural object.* Such that the Self is *Being*, it is that the Self is also capable of perceiving what is within the Self. The moment where a subject becomes in reflections on the concept, is precisely where language acts as the *designator* to things within the field of perception. It is as such that the field of experience reveals the transcendental dimension of reality to the Self upon its noetic pole (subjective). Through syntactical means alone, the observer finds available to consciousness, the inner sight prevails throughout the nature of Being in images of logical coordinates as transcendental experiences to a dialogical subject. It is, in this manner, that the univocity of the Self is actuated and the bifurcation between the objectified Self and its *noesis* becomes the reality of the subject.[9] Such that reference to events, places, subjects of interest, or historical moments are posited, the consciousness of the Self is transcendentally awakened by the phenomenality of *logos*. Insofar as Being is first universal to the understanding, the universality of the ordination of the field of actuality is also what bifurcates the objectivation to its intersubjective counterposition—the telos of humanity is particularized into the *observer* and the *observed*. Such that this moment is one where the phonology of discourse is apprehended intersubjectively, the conceptions that are represented to the other are universal to logos, yet particular to the understanding of the observed, now in the process of self-realization of an actuality that has come from the coordinates of the noematic pole of consciousness, where the Being of the Other is outwardly posited as speaking, i.e., the objective pole is listening to what is being said through phonological relation. It is in this manner that the transcendental understanding becomes of an oral tradition, despite psychoanalytic positions that these are disturbances *to* the Self—in effect the subject as Self has entered into a transformational process with the actuality of the perceptions themselves, of significations designated by speech as the *analogon* as signifier to *transcendental objective signification.*   In consideration of this conception of logos, it is rather that the objective world is the horizon of contemplation, persisting in transition from environmental coordinates that had generated the representation from the noematic pole, we necessarily concern ourselves with the distinction between the societal and the naturalistic, i.e., the conception of experience as conceptual to Being of its own nature, or conceptual to the societal context in which Being is understood to be particular to the conditions as opposed to the universal laws of nature. These are conceptions of the Self that are abstractions from the *historical cultural object*, and the *onto-teleological purposive object.*   The former is one produced by the dialectical processes generative of self-identification as the experience of subjectivity, within its social context from the standpoint of the awareness of justificatory rights provisional to a person based upon their prepossession of inalienable value as a resource to the political economy; and the latter is based upon a naturalization of the Being of Self, the self-concept as it exists of its own transcendental purposiveness that is universal to the becoming of the rational discourse necessary from the standpoint of the former being preserved within societal infrastructure.   The self-concept, unbound by the historical context in which the Self has come into Being, is problematic to the conception of what a self is, as both a social subject, and one that is purposive by its own naturalistic impetus to reproduce the transcendental coordinates of the nature of the Self. What concerns us most is that in order to function entirely based upon the natural rights that are posited by the understanding, judgment, and reason as Kant would have it, we are bound by the historical conception of what are the limitable provisional circumstances of the awakening that drives the self-concept from its conditional state of self-awareness where nature has been condemned through an absence of distributive justice throughout society—and therefrom the conception of Self is never quite possible in its innermost truthful form possible. It is as such that the historical context from which Being arises as a Self—in condemnation of the nature that had given it its purpose—is precisely the reason that the laws of the political economy themselves become forms delimiting the transcendental dimension to *Being*, as would further the awareness of the Self and the truthfulness of the reality of the purpose of existence; while facing an absence of a universality of context from where the conception of humanity may become of its own transformational activities—all to become the natural transformation of societies into what had been intended by the laws of nature, the only truthful universality that humanity has ever known. The objective world is one that is particular to the societal actualities of the syntactical context where cultural objectification has occurred, yet the natural impetus to become of a reality that is transcendental to the Self is part of the universality available to a transcendental nature exposed to Being, while ordered language is its very signification. It is such that the world is bifurcated into political science, and *natural* science. The objective world is within conception of the former, while the telos of species is the conception of the latter. Such as these are both coordinates available to human consciousness, their intersection and synthesis in thought is to be called the socio-naturalistic world. But what interests us here, is the conception of both society and nature as independently acting in terms of the coordinates of human activity, and reason in filiation with what propels a Self toward its own actuality and how dialogical positions may be universally bound by the societal context where they are existents of the universal genus of nature. The fact alone that language alone has evolved as a social construct elevates our discourse even further, since for *Being*, the conception of itself as closer to primitive actualities of our evolutionary past are not the coordinates that evoke the conception of what in fact the human Self might entail. How aren't we selves, and why are transcendental actualities foreign to the conceptions of Self as realities to be condemned due to their political instauration as deceptive forces of what might only signify the destructive powers experienced by generations past? Since the historical cultural object is particular to political science, and the telos of nature universal to human purposiveness, the matter will be further developed in the sequel, as the ordination of human purposiveness is elemental to the transcendental understanding, offering a quantum leap from where societies were first thought to be the source of all rational activity. Such that past generations have occasioned to witness planetary destruction, due to the conception of the historical context driving the order of the world forward, it is now that the process of establishing a new revolutionary context for humanity through which the order of nature is the *actuality* of humanity—as the source of what drives the transcendental understanding toward a horizon where the conception of a synthesis between society and nature is a universality of itself; once humanity is more awakened to the threshold of the transcendental understanding that is to revolutionize a conception of the world that bespeaks of the virtues of rational discourse; not as actualities based upon an infrastructure ethically bound to economic expansion, and less concerned with the substance of leisure without content. Such as it is, the conception of humanity as a universality of itself is identifiably incorrect, yet the conception of nature as the driving force unto humankind is more in keeping with the standardization of the values based upon an authenticity to purpose—that the rights associated with Being are those that are not only primordial ones, but also those that are significations that may be identified by natural science. The world as such is thought to be designed, as such, and the order of nature designated by the conceptions that accompany existing species upon the planet. To suggest that a Self may be a chimp, a dog, a rat, a mouse, a snake, a cockroach or a louse is an example of why the societal context that identifies humans in relation to other species is truthful to itself as an adulteration of the authentic teleological relation humans have to animals through natural science. Such that humans relate to animals as selves, so do animals relate to humans from the *telos* of nature into society and the totalization of society into nature or *societal nature*. Such that there is no universal conception of the latter, it is imposed upon a Self as a contingent articulation of an inherently flawed field of economic activity and is nothing transcendental. Such as it is this is the field of actuality where nominal judgments and name calling are identifiable as thought pollution, and never the consequences of justifiable or lawful claims. Insofar as nature is teleological, society is inherently dialectical in nature.[10] That the contingent articulation of the will of the other is only in appropriation of the actuality of an authentic transformation into an onto-teleological Being that is entwined with its own natural substance—the latter being the authentic onto-genetic content of Being that, upon horizons of productive activity, must be thought of as more viable than oversimplifications to actualities that are only a means to an end relative to the societal context wherethrough logic is biased toward cultural objects rather than those of an authentic universality of the genus of nature.

§1.4 *Being as essence and the transformation from subject to object (objective transformation).*
Being qua Being, or the existential conception that unites cognition with its expression in the self-concept as a verifiable organism, insofar as the former is able to perceive its own existence from the moment of conception to the moment of the idea in representation, signifies that the logic of the Self is inherent the modality of its expression in the experience of Self as *real*. Given the latter, the notion that one identifies oneself as such posits an object from the existing subject that is not identifiable as its proprietary expression of voluntary psychic experience. Such that this object intersects with corporeal being, it is that the object, as universal object of nature, is precisely what constitutes *essence*. In this sense, being is essence and essence is being. Both act as the logical coordinates of the self-concept, and compose the actuality of the subject. It is clear from this principle that this experience of the Self is what produces subjectivity as self-concept, and how the self-concept reproduces subjectivity as being and essence— therefrom opening the ontological landscape upon the noetic pole to the awareness of a horizon of activity that is both natural and transcendental. Such that it is a horizon of nature, it is phenomenal and empirical; and such that it is transcendental it is *phenomenological* and existential. As such the objects of nature are teleological objects, while the objects of the transcendental horizon are historical cultural objects. With this it is that the Self is of its nature through the sense of which the former defines the essence of the existence of the subject, while the latter determines the transcendental *episteme* of the context of experience where the universality of a subject may only be known through the universality of the *telos* of nature. As such the being of nature is precisely as it is of itself from its teleological origins, while the being of the self-concept as a transcendental abstraction, understands nature as something that is quite particular to subjectivity, rather than the universality of the genus of nature. In this sense, the conception of natural sense refers to this which constitutes reality

as a whole, while the transcendental constitutes reality in the particular sense—from subject to object, object to subject. As such the self-concept is represented both through a natural object that inheres of the subject, constituting the universal conditionality of subjectivity, while the transcendental object inheres of a subject as a representation that is as it is for Kant—either noumenal, or phenomenal. It is as such that Kant groups empirical objects with phenomena, but for the present purposes we must distinguish between the universal where concerns the purposive meaning of the self-concept, and the particular transcendental coordinates upon which phenomena are represented to a subject through phenomenological objects, symbolizations, noesis, retentive content, noema, and particular judgments, i.e. phonological and or representational contingencies.[11] As for the universality of noematic objects, it is that their concept remains universal, while their representation quite particular, given the transcendental reducibility of phenomenological content. A Self is itself only insofar as the conception of the former allows the Self as subject to be both conceived and posited as an object of the understanding—becoming an object that is phenomenological through a process where subjectivity transforms the natural object into its particularized Self as object—a conceptual self that is biased toward the horizon of its transcendental constitution. It is in this sense that the universality of the natural object becomes synthetic with the abstracted transcendental self-representation, only to become both the Being of nature, and the Being of the transcendental horizon—thus constituting both the universal within the particular and the particular within the universal. As such it is identifiable as transcendental nature. For the sake of argument, it is that the universality of genus is within the conception of nature but never the transcendental, in as much as things are particular to the episteme of the Self transcendentally, they are only universal as concepts, not as actualities acting as causal determinations of the performances underscoring the experiences of selves as subjects of a proprietary objective world. Such that the objects of the world are intelligible existences, they are particular to the Self as subject, and only universal insofar as they are particular to natural science. Such that things transcendental are particular as such, it does not exclude the Self from metaphysical contemplation, which is in-and-for-itself, based upon activities situated in historical and cultural norms—the act of prayers, meditations, onto-theological reflections, etc.

While Being for the sake of Being, of this existence, or of the objective natural world—what is it? For here the transformation from subject to object is something that might be unclear upon this juncture. What we know, is that the objective natural world is one where the universal teleology of nature provides an empirical context for where reality is hidden from the subjects within their own particularized self-identification. We also know that the historical cultural context of the transcendental understanding is signified to us with greater frequency, since the epistemological comprehension of Being is such that things such that they are known *a priori* are dimensions to contemplative activity that run the risk of falling away into misunderstandings and false beliefs. So, are we to take the conception that we have as a rational one, should the transcendental particularization of the Self possess a fixation that is rooted in the former without restriction—that Being is never to recognize its truth in the transcendental, as it had in the actualities that constituted the natural impetus to act by the Self as subject? It is only by and through objective transformation that it enters dimensions of possibility that the Self becomes as its own object—the natural and the transcendental object of a universality that has presented the analytic with the synthetic, the synthetic with the analytic. Such as there are no judgments in opposition to the conception of nature as a synthetic operation upon Being, we can certainly presuppose that the particularization of identity through the transcendental understanding is also self-identical, where the representation is rooted in its historical and cultural origins, and in this sense it is an appearance that is both truth of the Self, and self-identity to the Other as noematic object. With this it is that transcendental nature is both analytic and synthetic, where its constitution while immediate from a natural object, is synthetic once it has been mediated by the particularization of intersubjective beings.

As such there is an exchange between analytic and synthetic, while both are uncompromised between the pole of actuality and the necessary or contingent articulations that are posited between examined poles of consciousness. Such that humanity is transformed from subject to object, it is that both remain the former and the latter respectively through ontological bifurcation yet confer with one another as both the subjective analytic and the objective synthetic significations possible *a priori*.

§1.5 *Being transcendental subject—reflection as inherence in the act of representation and representation in the act of Being.*

Transcendental subjectivity posits the essence of being, disclosing itself contingently as an appearance that shadows a past, present, or a future Self while positing a *thing-in-itself.* It is just as easy to feel as Fichte had, under the duress of a free-acting, emancipatory rogue such as we become when the horizon of actuality is constituted by an historical cultural objectification. The point of the Self as transcendental subject, is to understand the nature of the Self—and lo and behold from the psychoanalytic stance, one might not always be pleased with the outcome. Such as the former constitutes the essence of a Self, it is that in effect this Self is not entirely yet quite itself, since it had previously been posited that the nature of the Self is generated by its teleological objectification. How then are we to weigh-in with the conception of transcendental nature, concerning the experience of the Self as transcendental subject? What has become quite clear is that the object to the Self is the actual Self, and the transcendental subject is precisely this which is other to its own purposive judgment. As we cannot have purpose without pairing it with judgment, we must also accommodate the sense of what is in human nature of purpose, must also be in human nature of judgment. It is in this sense that *meaning* becomes possible, as one applies it to the self-concept and realizes what is truth to self-identification. Through acts of reflection, what inheres of a subject is precisely the reflexive accommodation of a representation to the self, such that the reproduced activities of the self-identical are posited as judgments and the dialectical reasoning that yields the ordinance of Being as existent to the field of actuality—a landscape where transcendental nature stands a chance of spatializing representations of universality, rather than the contingent natures of those that have been mediated by the differentia posited by particularized beings in objective disunification. Universality as it stands as the genus of the teleological manifold, where intersections between objectivated entities manifestly litter the space of representation with opposing political factions, presents a problem to the question of whether metaphysics is still a possibility—in consideration of the concept of human nature. Reality is constituted by the facts themselves, it is not a horizon of ill-conceived falsities concocted in order to manipulate minds into positions of tacit obedience. Yet if it is suggested that the actuality of humanity is its natural existence, how then will I come to face the problem this presents where the onto-genetic presentations of selves consistently find themselves at loggerheads; and willing to go to battle for the territory where the universal may be legislated by one administrative body or another. Such that the expressions of Self as transcendental subject are eminently representations that propose to identify subjects as struggling with the differences proposed by their very universal conception, it is that we undertake to comprehend or to apply the transcendental understanding to a reality that appears upon the horizon as the natural expression of human conduct, before it has been particularized by the historical cultural framework where the transcendental horizon is its generative component. The position of the latter is representative of the reproduced elements of societal infrastructure as well, as their historical and cultural context is the primary signification of how actualities of transcendental subjects will be carried out. That these self-generating representations inhere of a transcendental subject, provides the grounds for a transformation of the appearance to the Self, as the representations of Being are transcendentally reflexive between self-identical subject and object. Appeals to the reproducibility of the horizon in this way capacitates abstractions of transcendental phenomena, while the ego is transcendentalized becoming an actuality to the self-concept in pursuit of empirical justification as an authentic being of nature. The act of Being—in as much as it is the actuality of the Self, is in this manner within justification as a transcendental subject where the horizon is one that is constituted by needs, and by proclivities of the natural substance of the transcendental subject. It is in this way that humanity is both transcendental and natural and posits a Self upon the transcendental horizons of nature.

§1.6 *Nature as Transcendental Consciousness and the reciprocity of the understanding.*
The teleology of humans is such that horizons to the understanding posit propositions and judgments underlying conceptions of subjects as part of the transcendental consciousness, where the understanding had first encountered its historical and cultural contextualization. What is posited within conception is the conditionality of objects inhering subjective transcendental reflection—the very praxis that defines transcendental consciousness as a totality to the human understanding. Such that the being of nature is transcendental, once it has become particularized to its own

signification as identical to the environmental conditions that had conditioned the Self, it forms what constitutes the structure of belief. This constitutes the relational modality of self-identity—both structured and natural, that the responses to the natural and the synthetic environment have given the Self its truth and own formal causality from effect. It is in this manner and by these very means that transcendental self-identity becomes both natural to the Self just as it does become transcendental to the natural environment in which the Self actuates its natural determinations and reflexive judgments. So it is that the Self is both self-identical in nature and transcendentally self-identical. As such the self-concept forms the reality of *Being* and expresses what is true *to* form for transcendental reflection, into an understanding Self as transcendental subject and empirical object to others as discovered through signifiers that are neither empirical nor transcendental.

§1.7 *Representations and signifiers to an object that has no subjective signifying function.*

Insofar as there are natural objects, historical cultural objects, objects of knowledge, etc., the material objects of the world would seem to possess signifiers coincident with the praxis involving quotidian activities constitutive of subjective actualities. In effect this is the essence of Being— the object upon which one, whether at work or play, is consistently interacting, that has for it both representation and is signified from other rectilinear coordinates outside of the *in situ* architectonic environment. It will be necessary to define the difference between the signifying powers of the representation and the signifier, however. A representation, is thought to be merely a thought function, identifying an object or thing that is posited without reference to any object or signified upon the field of actuality. Whereas a signifier corresponds with an object that is other to the signified, while precisely the Being which is signified only through the identification of rectilinear coordinates from where the signification had been projected. It is quite clear that this is something transcendental as an existent of the political economy, where all such activities that constitute the production of content may be situated. Objects, such that they are reproduced in this way, offer modal relations to the input and output of creative activities and the positing of *Being*—rather than the experience of an absence of reproductive actuality—necessitating a stand-still arising of revolutionary mindfulness in pursuit of the object of one's most profound attainment of needs. The sensible datum that evokes within us the conceptualization of a reality that is neither real nor ideal, neither natural nor transcendental, but the very coordinates from where the mind is compelled to actuate existence as an authorship of a reality to which no things natural or transcendental stand in opposition—if so, dialectically neutralized. It is in this way that the soul of humanity is preserved and activated as a source of truth, justice, honour, and judgment—a horizon which composes the naturalization of self-identity from its roots in the teleological dimension of its primordial self-awareness—the motivational force driving transcendental nature forward thus, toward its symbolization as a more fortuitous potency than what were conceived where the landscapes of human actuality were dominated by an indifference to the authenticity of the totality of the positions from where the justification of this life resounds in its most significatory manner possible.

§1.8 *Being phenomenal identity as signification—the signifying function of the empirical Self.*

The Self is identical to itself and thus is identical in nature as a Self as were previously noted. As such the self-concept is one that is empirical to the self as is posited by the natural reproducibility of Being from the existential concept of Being from its horizons of origination. The question regarding the precise coordinates of this horizon, finds reasonable origins in the primordial essence of humanity, as a horizon of actuality that is posited by existence of a totality of species that have come into existence as a function of an organic unification of planetary substance and the universality of the genus of species, known to humanity of an evolutionary praxis determined by the Earth's orbit around the sun and the provisions made possible to planetary life, through the cosmogenic atmosphere that produces and reproduces life forms at a differential rate to how rapidly species reach the point of extinction. As the objects of the *planosphere* respond to the natural order as derived by the intelligibility of natural events determining and determined by human activities, *Being* may reconcile experience with existence so as to posit the former as a phenomenon—therethrough rendering self-signification as identical and real to the experience of the Self, within its logical structure as a natural essence—thereto the experiential Being of an empirical Self. Such that this natural component of the psyche is part of the episteme of the subject, it is that the positions of the Self are transcendental; and insofar as they make reference to the logical self, they are natural components to the primordial expressions of Being that underscore the historical context where the existential Self has recognized its existence by and through the others, throughout the intelligibility of the logical coordinates where self-identity realizes the truth that is intelligible to modal relations. As such the horizons of intelligibility are these from which the reality of a self as subject that is existentially entwined with its own phenomenality is conceptual to the experience of the phenomenon as an empirical existent that has been posited upon the coordinates of the transcendental nature of Being, as it recognizes the magnitude of truth that composes objective self-identification as the reality upon the threshold of the becoming of Being as a transcendental natural phenomenon. This as an entity is only apportioned to the transcendental and the *ideal,* or the natural and the *real* insofar as the empirical Self has not yet become of the truth that were posited by the naturalization of its own universal identification as a transcendental existential phenomenon. Where the coordinates of the experience of this phenomenon are first posited may be reconciled only insofar as the primordial expressions to the Self are upon the locus of judgment where the abstractions possible to transcendental subjectivity are also first the natural onto-genetic proclivities, determining perceptual capacitation and the potencies of the faculty of cognition. One is either fruitful or fruitless in pursuit of what is dynamical to the Self, as possible to abstraction from the loci of activity where Being discovers the anthropological necessities that are universal to the primordiality of Being through the naturalization of the societal restrictions upon the conditionality of the Self as subject.

In this way, the Self is an entity that is first posited in its own nature but must reconcile with the existential horizons of Being in order to become of self-identical truth as both natural and transcendental. For this reason, the phenomenal Self is a synthesis of its natural analytic empirical Self and the transcendental existential Self. The purpose of self-realization then becomes the meaning conditional to a subject imposed by the reconciliation between the natural proclivities that identify the Self as subject and the societal context wherethrough a Self is posited as logical relative to other such subjects, both driven by nature and by the coordinates of its own transcendental self-identification. Inasmuch as the universality of genus is composed of a plurality of beings that are not logically accessible to transcendental nature, one must only realize the potential from where the greed of others inheres of self-seeking subjects awaiting their natures to determine the evil acts that they suggest are never to be met with the consequences of either natural or transcendental laws that would revoke the status of some from the ideal reality of any proposition such as this.

To reason with what are the dynamics of natural laws, we must first posit what is *real* to cause and what is *ideal* in effect. For transcendental laws we must posit what is *ideal* to cause and what is *real* in effect. Nature, as a series of substances comprising the elements of all bio-scientific actuality, possesses its unmistakable reality as is readily diagnosable through observation of its existing phenomena, and is causal to the actualities of primordial humanity as species-beings, otherwise determined through the effects of societal environmental conditions that are purposive to humans only insofar as the particularization of universal substance has been transcendentalized into a state of conditional historical or cultural flux. The causes of nature are real to humanity as they are in our natural planetary habitat, and also the generating force upon primordial being as existence undergoes its natural determinations and realizes them through the ideality of its own effects—that what is requisite is immediate and must not necessarily be questioned, lest reflexive self-identification between nature and existence is developmental of effects that are posited as counter to nature, or logically biased toward a causal transcendental ideality. The existential horizon where humanity endeavors to perceive itself as a universality of possibilities, has not yet attained the goal, as it is first of an utmost necessity that Being is realized as identical to its own nature and not the transcendental positions of those acting within biases that are ideal to cause, i.e. the transcendental self has not yet encountered the being of nature. It is precisely this Being that is the existent before the industrialization of the previous two centuries and realizes itself upon the natural coordinates of its own judgment.[12] Such that this historical process undermined the natural developmental coordinates of the horizons of actuality, where the bio-genetic purposiveness of humanity would have reached its full potential—a measure of the magnitude of the universality of genus as the reified substance of species-beings—the motive to change the determinations imposed by nature, or to supplant them with societal conditionalities that unnaturally transform subjectivity from its originary patterns of behaviour, is an assault upon what is ideal in effect—that humanity will evolve in a natural way, realizing that scientific discovery is not only about economic trends or radical movements in aesthetics, but rather that these are equally possible while remaining true to form—in full possession of what is real to cause. What is necessary to humanity is the reality of existence, as we are primordial in essence and ontological in existence. What is real to the Self as an ontological Being, must be realized through its phenomenal self-identification as immanent to the Self, not something real that is abstract to the Self through dialectical transformation. That the transformation of humanity toward the self-realization of a significatory empirical Self—blessed with a reality that is generated through the natural process of self-realization, from the natural laws determining the immanence of Being upon the locus of its transcendental nature thus, is a logical horizon upon which the extensions of thought reason toward a dialectical anthropology, necessitating the form through which reality is shaped by an effectuation of the ideality of its own effects. The immanence of nature within its transformability as an empirical Self is the Being of its own essence—the actuality of its own substance.

§1.9 *Transcendental aesthetics in contingency to natural objects of the Self.*

That Being is immanent, it is also transcendental as it is natural.[13] The empirical Self is an object of itself that is both natural as it is phenomenal, through the elements that compose the substance of organic nature. Such that the experience of Being is the reality of itself through the synthesis between the transcendental and the natural, the empirical self becomes of itself through the universality of genus and the transcendental horizon that particularizes subjectivity, such that the existential calibrations of the Self are posited through the self-concept, as the process of self-realization through the historical biological context generating the transformation from subject to natural object is generated by the active necessitation of the logical coordinates to Being—determining the actuality that is posited upon the locus of judgment where the analytic a priori Self is the natural object of its universal self-experience. Boundaries to the Self are those that are cast beyond the limitation from its natural coordinates thus, and the object in its transformative capacitation of the natural existential subjectivity encounters the spiritualization of the natural object to the Self—realizing that Being is composed of both its natural object and the transcendental existentiality of its subjective objectivation. With this, actuality is realized where the particular is subsumed beneath the universal and the locus of its particularization returns to a generalization of that is transcendental to the experience of reality, as the context from which all conceptions of the Self are first posited. As such, the necessary, or natural object of the Self, as the universality of the being of the self-concept, is contrasted with the contingent, or transcendental horizon of the Self that is abstracted once the process of unmediated self-identification has posited the logical coordinates of the abstract Self from its transcendental horizontal instauration as the historical cultural reality to *Being*. As the Being of necessity is universal to the self-concept, the being of contingency is particular to self-identification, and thus the particularization of subjectivity happens to posit the transcendental coordinates of the Self in contingency. These are thus also natural to the logical existentiality of the loci from where such aesthetic objects may be abstracted, and thus the symbolic imagination may posit such coordinates thereby creating a logical structure to the determinable coordinates of the ontological nominalization of synthetic actuality.[14]

Given that the meditative praxis of the Self constitutes transcendental aesthetics in such a manner as to posit the lifeworld in contingency, with the natural object of the Self as its universalization, it becomes possible to actualize the transcendental phenomena through psychic realities—as experiences that are logically contingent; yet none the less constitutive to the reality of the natural existential horizons upon which the Self becomes itself of and through itself. The methodization of positing the Self as a natural object with existential coordinates must be generative of the transcendental phenomena particular to the Self—thereby upon the landscapes of noetico-noematic contemplation we become of the *idea* in property relations just as we had previously in modal relations that had instantiated the determinability of the contemplative activities that constitute happenings upon the field of actuality. To suggest that these are imaginary coordinates within conception of a delusional Self are positions often held in psychoanalytic theory, but we now know that the representations themselves are merely the grounding of the objects as they exist upon the logical coordinates from where such quantum realities may be architectonically represented to the human mind. That they are in contingency is more to the point and, as such, has created the conception of the image consciousness having no grounding in the realities of quotidian existence. What we see might not always be acceptable to the realities of ordered societies, but nonetheless is truth to the Self in that moment of existential self-actualization. Quite particular to aesthetic theory is the conception that the human mind is in possession of cognitive faculties that are no longer in use due to the technological revolutions of the past several decades; but we must persevere such that the transcendental dimensions of reason may reach their ultimate goal in synthesis between the natural object and the transcendental phenomena thus. What is natural to Being in logical transformation is its universality; and what is transcendental to existence is its transformability as is posited of the human condition, that is both one of universality in necessity and particularity in contingency. It is thus that the being of seeing is natural to the conceptions of Self where the seeing of Being is transcendental to the existential experience of the Other.

Chapter 2

Intelligence, as it at first recollects the intuition, places the content of feeling in its own inwardness—in a space and time of its own. In this way that content is an image or picture, liberated from its original immediacy and abstract singleness amongst other things, and received into the universality of the ego. The image loses the full complement of features proper to intuition, and is arbitrary or contingent, isolated, we may say, from the external place, time, and immediate context in which intuition stood.—Hegel

§2.1 *Being and Seeing.*

In the necessity of the universality of natural Being, the contingency of the image is what is posited through the abstraction upon the transcendental horizon, from where it had been generated in temporal suffusion from the locus of actuality where it is harnessed thus; as what is symbolic to the mind, and realized as a contingent reality to the Self. Inasmuch as the Self receives this symbolization from its generative capacitation in contingency, the methodization from which the natural synthetic calibration of ontological experience is inward the psyche as the being of itself, in-and-for-itself, is posited as the truth of the contingent necessitation of the external coordinates from where the abstract Self had posited a Self as itself, and become through the emptiness of its own self-concept.[15] This opening of the Self to the experiences of other intelligible realities, is particular to the substance of modal relations, insofar as the Self is ideational toward its transcendental horizon thus, and contemplative within a logic that is comprehensible to the conception of the Self as an equal logical coordinate to the inception of the Other as its logical counterposition in contingent reality. The naturalization of the Self from its objectification, as composed of its uncalibrated psychical Being-for-Self, is actuated in the recompense from where natural being identifies the Self as identical to itself, through and of its own natural proclivities as are determinable of ego-identification—through the universalization of symbolic identification upon the coordinates of the vertical instantiation of identical presuppositions, posited within the personalization of the transcendental ego upon the locus of judgment, into a self-positing thing-in-itself—thus departing the vision of the Other as intelligible and rendering consciousness void an identification of the Self as its Other—or the Other as Self, inward the gaze of reality to Being and the transcendental dimension to one's *universality* in identification.

Insofar as the Self is the understanding self, it is that the universality of the Self is natural to the symbolization of itself, and transcendental to the symbolization of its Other. The self as self, is of itself and other to the symbolization, and therefrom is actual to a dimension of consciousness from the self-consciousness that had been activated through the nullification of the emptying of the Self into itself, as the logical proximation from which the transcendental coordinates of the intelligible beings posited upon horizons of experience would become envisioned in abstraction. Where encounters with Others therefrom are transcendental, they are not yet natural to the Self, and where they are *natural* to Self they are not yet transcendental to Others. Not until the process of nominal symbolization has occurred do propositions or judgments constituting horizons upon which all seeing becomes possible to the naturalization of the Self, do we realize the potency of the realities presupposed by what is natural to the genus determinable to the universalization of the Self as an object to Other intelligible nominal Beings. Upon the threshold of symbolization, the immanence of ego identification of the Self as Other to symbolic instantiation, presupposes the modality of transsubjective relations as inhere of the dialectical, anthropic medium-of-exchange that proposes the ultimation of the aestheticization of the sign as a captured object to the naturalization contextualized through its logical formalization. We are thus, transformed, by and of self-identity, through the abstraction from the coordinates wherefrom the subjective instauration of the image object is posited as the real identity toward the positing of the symbol as a particular signifying component of the psychical manifold, more prone to posit Being as abstract, than as the natural presupposition of its syntactical verisimilitude—a simulacrum from which syntactical formalizations are posited as realities to dreamers and wisdom-seeking sorcerers alike. As the universe will undeniably open to such wayfarers of the landscapes altogether restricted the modality of an unconscious dominion over high-minded, individuated soul-seekers, propositional to the context wherethrough a mindful consciousness is aesthetically entwined within the ideation of a private universe, unbound by the forms through which adequate judgment has been reconciled within the content of its own form, it is thoughtful of Being to realize the context in which logical symbolic content is to be reconciled within aesthetic judgments—*ergo* we are being and seeing with an intentionality that has been reasoned from an authentic position in reasoning, i.e., something that has otherwise gone undisclosed must be revealed to a Self within the context of its own ethical transformation as determinable of the necessary processes wherethrough the truth would become of the universal, rather than of a particular contingency that had undermined the universal in pursuit of a privative pecuniary interest. Where the city meets the soul of humanity, is likely the same place where the landscapes of being were sense-certainties underlying civil disputes, deploying a naturalization of the necessary contingencies as set conditions to the judgments posited by the authentication of a nature-driven self-conceptualization inhering as the object of a symbolization determinable of an unmediated universality that has yet to encounter its own horizon.

§2.2 *Being extension.*

The world in which we live is made-up of logical coordinates situated at the locus of actuality where the contemplation of people, places and things brings rise to thoughts that are projected to the loci where the Self is in extension thus.[16] That one may be positive that the natural responses from these loci are real and may be symbolized to the Self, is a reasonable presupposition to make, for what other representations must one have such that the positions from which the Self as object is universal to particular points in time and space must one have? It would be easy to dismiss these proprietary imaginings as mere possibilities, but once they have been verified it would seem that the transcendental *episteme* has been delivered, such that the coordinates of our own social imaginary is lost to the ideals of the experience of one for whom the relativity of all possibilities is more absolute than an ontological happening. As with Descartes—the progenitor of the rectilinear logical coordinates in revelatory salutation of what we might know as transcendental egos—we salute you fair fellow, for how much further must we travel in order to substantiate what in appearance have rationalistic verifiability throughout the results of those for whom extensions to being seem all-too-lofty to be acknowledged by us *in toto*? Such as it would seem, these are the extensions of Self, they are the de facto projections from the core of experience, toward the horizons of our own actualities—substance in equal measure to the reification of our own object of thought as an adjunct to the distantiation that is held within us—across the lacuna to the proximities where the vision we have of ourselves becomes a necessity to the cause; as is particular to the effectuation of what gathers conceptions of Being from their own locus of judgment toward the processual point of access and of the potency of a return to the Self that is the beyond of its own field of actuality, and the substantiation of the existentiality of its positional stance as a natural and enduring spiritual edifice of productively active contemplation.

§2.3.1 *Being reflection.*

The actuality of Being is the universality of its reflective activities and the retentive capacitation that goes unbridled throughout the reasoning that is engaged through meditative practices—it is only through the dynamics of how one produces themselves as a subject that we must here concern ourselves, for we are, after all, a Self as subject. Such that we are a Self, we reflect upon the object of thought—which is known to us through reflective activities and therewith, the objects of interest are those that may be retained through the imagination, memory, and perceptual insight (which is available to the more gifted or educated in symbolic logic and mathematics). The extensions to the Self, offer the mind in thought a representation of objects occurring in space and time, and it is these that we know to be the very objects of interest to us. If we begin by positing a conception of a named object, it becomes of an appearance—given the faculty of representation is optimally functional. If we wish to perceive a specific object that we already know to exist, we must simply possess the knowledge of the locus of actuality where we might presuppose said object to exist i.e., a city, street, building, person of interest—Behold! one had already arrived upon the threshold of the retentive memory. Using the imagination to accomplish this is one of the tools that is quite useful, put otherwise, things that may be perceived symbolically are abstract or posited in this manner, and by these means alone may become part of the development of a reflective retentive memory. Apart from this, the actuality of coordinates may also be within reason accessible to the Self, as the dialectical exposition of the possibility of a subject-object existing in space and time becomes of logical propositions to the judgments proposed through activated reflection. In order not to mistake phantasy for reality, one must first possess the knowledge of one object in particular, then posit it beneath a universality of conditions that reduce it to its most visible formal content. In this way it is both conceivable as an actuality, and an actuality in conception.

§2.3.2 *Being judgment.*

Insofar as objects are abstracted or posited by *mind*, we may judge them. But in order to abstract them, a proposition must already have been posited upon the locus of where objects may be judged and/or perceived. As a Self, I perceive as a judge, throughout what is natural to Being, I posit: this is a beautiful mountain. I observe the foliage and find myself realizing nature's colourful bounty and resplendence. I do not posit: "Humans are scum!",— even though the experience of many atomized individuals would lead one to believe that they are. The Self as subject is just that, a *Being*. Something that is having a picture of the world in mind that is realizing what in effect it signifies. Such that the represented object gives pleasure, it is beautiful; and such that the represented object gives pain, it is hideous. It is really that simple. But I digress, as the willingness to posit that things should not be judged as they are, once the gaze has penetrated through the deceptions of appearances into the possibility that there might be some shred of compassion or kindness within—a radiance of spiritualized inner beauty that glows from the core of an inner truth—we find the Self immersed within the search for a reality that fulfills the expressions of human experience—such that we yearn for nothing more than an abstraction of a raison-d'être that resides within the Self as universal to nature, yet altogether particular to well-being. The phenomena of humankind are such that the association between a Self and the disengaged objects that we have allowed to fall away—rising to the edge of their own reified loss of the beauty that might have been achieved—posit that there are no judgments that must be endured until the truth is an object of reality.

§2.4 *Being and universality.*

The being of Self experiences a universality of self that is deployed from nature as its generative capacitation, and authentic substance. As the positing Being is primordial to subjectivity, it is within the logic of humans to propose that Being is as it is in-and-of-itself, for-and-in-itself. Such that this universality is the mere expression to the manifold understanding that humans possess reason *a priori*, and must not be concerned with the positions of Others being situated in logical possibility to the positing of the human element composed by the naturalization of primordial rights, we dialectically subvert inauthenticity for the purposes of realizing the truth of substantively modal relations in an effort to subjugate the will of the Other beneath the composition of a more fertile and authenticated actuality to the proposed universal context through which reality must reach its adequation.[17] Of lore, the tides are turning and a blessed infamy of forgotten generations has capitulated its stance within the experiences of the souls of those that were lost amidst the hatred and violence that had been perpetrated by the abhorrent behaviours that disassembled the logic of those for whom the evolution of human consciousness has not even begun to blaze the trail—toward what we in effect had actuated upon the reprisal of the happening of the potentialities that furthered the meaning of this existence—into a core reality that were less forgotten than any messianic comprise would ever have afforded. The universality of what is natural to humanity is at stake, less the destruction of our habitat becomes what the origins of our species might have meant by the conceptions of industry culture, as having been more biased toward a destructive capacitation of a quite unwelcome residency upon the suffusion of the planet into a profanity more unjust than existential crises that had delivered it as a force of nature—less vital than the transformations of the Self into its most significant modal reality as had first been posited by actualities proposing a societal model composed of the conception of more equality, a constitutional protectorate purposive to needs of citizens and justice for all.

§2.5 *Being and particularity.*

The being of Self becomes particular once it has reified the transcendental coordinates of the historical and cultural positions posited upon the existential horizon of its own actualities in reproduction. A Self as itself, is this being that is the *Being* particular, and notices that the societal context wherethrough the possibilities of existence are reified in the context where they are only made so through social relations in possession of control and influence of the dynamics that govern the viability of a subject *vis-à-vis* the ultimate position that one is to occupy within the former. Where one is *particularized*, one has been more responsive to the a priori conditions as imposed by nature as the authentic objectification of primordial Being. Where one has been universalized from the particular—an experience of the Self wherethrough social relations have more actively posited the conditions to the subject through customs and cultural norms, the subject has come to identify the truth to their own natural essence—thereto becoming self-identical to the reality of their own existence, as in full possession of the necessary rights to justify a natural transformation of the Self toward the horizons of what is actual to Being; therewith in discovery of the authenticity of modal relations, such that the absence of the disclosures of the past bereft this authenticity had posited a horizon of truth to the Self as subject.

§2.6 *Being and Totality.*

The being of Self becomes total once it has realized its conception in the synthesis between the natural object and the transcendental horizon that had been unified with the object of nature through its universalization thus into the singularity of transcendental nature. A total Self as subject is singular in totality, while universal in singularity—a Being of perfection once the historical and cultural classification of its transcendental Self has been mediated by the natural universality that had first been posited in and throughout the Self. As such, reality, is the Self of itself, the nature-giving composition of the Self as both natural and transcendental, transcendental and natural. In this way, the totality of Being is within the Self as subject and a reality to existence; and a spiritual revitalization that is posited both within the natural and the synthetic habitat of the essential core experience to planetary self-realization. The self-concept is itself, and the totality of Self upon the horizons of existence where Being realized the truth of its own experience in totality—the totality of its own experience. It is so that *Being* is natured toward the Self as an existent of the totality, and the totality an existent to the Self. The immanence of totality is such that the

Self is its own totality, and the totality of immanence is such that it is a totality of the Self. We are one in totality, and a totality of one, as Being is the totality of the existence of one and the existence of the one of totality. Where the Self is in the becoming of its own singularity, it is total in singularity; and where singularity is in the becoming of the self, it is singular in totality—a total Self. Such that Being is of itself and total to the Self, it is a self in totality—it is a real singularity that its totality has been posited by the transcendental horizon of its natural becoming; and such that the Self is of this Being, it is that the Self is total to the singularity and has been posited by the natural objectification of a universalized transcendental horizon.

§2.7.1 *Being cause.*

Insofar as there is a cause for being, being may also be causal. The cause for being is natural and the being of cause is transcendental. As such, there are natural causes and transcendental causes. Natural causes are *generative*, and *determinative*, while transcendental causes are *preemptive* and *presentative*. Where natural causes are posited by the understanding, it is necessary for the Self to judge the object of the cause, such that the outcome is not one that is *accidental*. Where transcendental causes posit a representation, it is necessary for the Self to employ thought in order choose what is necessary, while reflecting upon the propositional content within the transcendental understanding. Being is identical to itself in nature and causes that are natural are identical in necessary phenomena, while the causes that are transcendental are identical in contingent noumena. Humanity is a cause in-and-of-itself and as such is both through the historical cultural context of its coming into being a causal force upon the planet within the universal, such that transcendental causes intersect with natural ones through prior ontological conceptions of what is in both cause and effect in transcendental nature. Transcendental causes—based within habitualities, rituals, and organizational practices—act upon and within nature to impose upon Earth an order to the political economy that is apportioned to the transcendental horizon upon which the universality of nature orders existence in such a way as to find a particularization of subjects that are both particular and universal to the *causal reflex*. As such causality is reflexive, or to be identified as reflexive causality, and thereto the source of many undesirable outcomes that are both generative and determinative through the synthesis of the transcendental with nature. So it is that Being qua Being is both causal and caused, and it is in this way that what is functional to our societies must be something that is caused rather than causal, such that there has been an intervention that has led to a more favourable outcome than the one that has been generated by the fluxion of the transcendental horizon to the understanding—more prone to accept the results, due to the historical or cultural context within which the event had taken place. It is in this way that Being Cause is natural to humanity, as the order of nature is universal to the conception of humans as species in full possession of the survival instinct, and thereto able to transform the world around them from their primordial nature, using the tools that have become available to us through the realization of ourselves in the transcendental context where the origins of praxis as communities in science and the arts have been generative of an order to nature, that within reason, may yet be preserved—though we cannot turn back the clock and the destructive powers of our transcendental nature will only respond through interventions of a collective intelligibility that must organizationally reform the administrable societies in which we live—toward a horizon where the reality of our transcendental nature is precisely an object of the will that is Being Cause; never the cause of death and destruction, but only this which nullifies the positional stance we have taken upon the planet of a spiritual awakening that has obfuscated the boundaries of reason, reducing us to a mere shadow of the former presentation of the human soul as something real to the cause, through a nature than has evolved beyond the primitivity of generations past; resulting in an order to nature that has been lost in misunderstanding and the dissolution of a projection of humanity that would be the cause—the natural cause—of a transcendental revolution that would change all conceptions of meaning toward a more fecund landscape of human endeavor than what we had left behind of the twentieth century.[18] To suggest that the monsters of the last hundred years or more were beings of nature, is an attempt to not look at the conception of the transcendental through the lens of its historical, cultural, and scientific relativity. Humankind was born to prosper upon this planet, just not at the hands of the ones whom continuously seem to amass enough power to control the political economy with their killing machinery. The immediacy of our transcendental nature must be the cause of the effects and the effects of our own ethical causes—lest the destruction of nature comes to destroy us all in the end.

§2.7.2 *Being effect.*

Insofar as Being has its effects, there is also an effect *for* Being. The effect for being is natural, while being in effect is transcendental. Natural effects are reflexive and accidental, while transcendental effects are controlled and administrable. The effects of transcendental nature, however, are much more prone to a radical transformation than the ones proposed by either nature in its effects, or transcendental effects. As such, effects are dialectical in nature, and rhetorical as transcendental. Where the Self is itself, as itself—the very nature of itself in its own effect, it is transcendental and self-identical, and where the Self is of itself in-and-for-itself a transcendental being, it is natural and non-identical. In discovery of the process whereby a mind is of transcendental nature it is both necessary and phenomenal and noumenally contingent. Alas, we live with the effects of the causes that have been posited by the Self, and at the hand of the understanding of Other Beings for whom the Self may come to the point of understanding by way of pure reason alone. In the historical context from which the transcendental dimension to active contemplation had been developed, we have four centuries of working and warring toward a transcendental horizon of our own expectations. In this sense effects are more historical than the causes themselves. It is by these means that the transcendental effects, such as they are, are the results of causes that were more historically charged as had been posited prior. We are the effects of both historical cultural causes and natural ones. It is suggested that the historical context wherefrom a Self is presentative to itself and is a cause to its own effect, is precisely the position where the context that is posited by being is singular to the transformation that has occurred from within the Self—as a Being of passive contemplation—situated between cause and effect and Being effect rather than cause. And where the Self is in its nature wherefrom a Self is determinative of itself and is an effect to its own cause, is precisely the position where the dialectical impetus that is projected by Being is universal to the transformation that will occur within the Self, as a Being of active contemplation—situated between cause and effect and Being cause rather than effect.

§2.7.3 *Effects as causes and causes as effects.*

Insofar as there is correspondence between effects and causes, causes and effects, these reside in the natural world through most of the crises that have occurred in the last several decades, no less. The global impacts of climate change and the pandemic at the top of the list—throughout the tumult of wars and insurrection—during the developmental waste of a political economy that has departed its position in sense-certainty for a residency in the stratosphere as a companion to jettisoned dreams and idling dignitaries, floating through desperate moments of poor choice and bad decision making—we are the effects of the causes and the causes of the effects. Through passive contemplation, historical determinability had led humanity down a dark path, toward the obfuscation of a subversion of the rationalistic ideals of those that throttled toward the horizon of a forgotten idealism. Through active contemplation, universal self-determinability engaged the thoughts of disinterested sycophants that gloated over the destructability of a more intelligible humanity than the one that had been proposed by the disparate reasoning of ill-fated congregations, unnamed due to their ownership of a despoiled conception of what perpetuated a horizon only identifiable as an arrival upon the shores of an attainable recompense from where the notion that we were fated for more were undeniable—mad at the heels of a lost and dying breed of hegemonic interlocutors, muddling toward the horizon of an dissembled realism. Where we—the generation that had been denying ourselves as the ones for whom acceptance were a flagrant impossibility, as the fledgling souls awaiting the moment of justice to arrive—would be more prone to appropriate meaning than teeter upon the realities that were proposed by those for whom access to dissent would only be awarded to the shortest, most virulently opposed to reason; offenders to judgment that had been within the conception of the beings of the natural universe that proposed that we would find our purpose within a suffusion into the constitutive loss that had warranted a provisional disillusionment forward thus. It is us, the effect of the cause, the cause of the effect that projects for more than what were possible—only to discover less than what were conceivable. It is in this moment that the effects are natural, and the causes transcendental. It is in this moment that the meaning is dialectical, and the obfuscation of our purpose rhetorical. Within abstraction is reality within conception, the purposive meaning of an abandoned past that has been reified only through an historical meaning that must be interpreted before it confers with a vulnerability that has yet to present itself in innocence. A conception of the human species that is determinable of itself and to itself—perceiving horizons that are congregations of the meanings that have been conceived through their own interpretation.

§2.8 *Being sustainability.*

Historical causes have effects, just as effects have historical causes. Natural causes have effects, just as there are effects that are caused by nature—both natural phenomena and the natural objects of human nature. As such, the object of humanity is to preserve ourselves however we can—to subsist within and of the causes, and to exist within our own effects and create the causes of our own transformation thus. The question as to what is sustainable to humankind requires a lengthy and profound treatment that will only be briefly touched upon here. Humanity—from inception, to self-conception, throughout the evolutionary development of reason and forward toward both planned and unplanned arrivals in desecration of the environment whilst ever-pursuing the objective of a horizon for human consciousness never to be lost on our species; we disappear within appearances and appear within the disappearance of the reason that we had become the necessities through provisions and become provisional through our own necessities—all-the-while becoming contingent to our necessities and in toleration of contingent necessities while promoting free-will as the very instrument of our own salvation. Why do we war in the search for things that are destructive to humanity, and search for wars that are humanity's very destruction, such that the transformation of Being toward horizons of discovery would be biased toward a change that were necessary to existence rather than contingent to non-existence? This world is a world of its own nature—the natural world, as such. What is sustainable is within the grasp of those that are willing to participate in the vision for humanity that is universal in nature—within the singular potential of each living citizen that has it within them to gaze into an awakening that posits a galvanized and forward thinking machinery in perpetuation of the realities that constitute a moment in time that is self-sustaining, self-determining, and self-actualized through the judgments that are natural to the human condition once they have been transcendentalized; and nature-sustaining, nature-determining, and naturally actualized through the judgments that are transcendental to nature—given that the realities of this planet are objective in nature, and natural objectives of the Beings in occupation of the planet Earth. As such transcendental nature is within conception a reproduction of a planned political economy, biased toward the universality of nature as its very conception and objective mode to developmental reason, unhinged by the notion that the compromise of the natural, environmental habitat is not a constitutive loss, but one that we cannot afford to witness within the space of time that we have left to actuate the reconfiguration of administrable forces, such that the residency within the nucleus of human activity is not a pollutive effect with destructive powers to the psyche—just as it has constructive powers to the ego that undermine the causes that are propositional, dialectical positions to the will that are natural to transformative capacitation; underlying biases in reformation of the controlled effects that dominate transcendental nature within the emancipatory conception of a nature, unhinged by the reflexivity between nature and the transcendental thus.   With this, it is that the neutralization of pure transcendental conceptions becomes a necessity to humanity, throughout an exposition of meaning that decries a realism that is never within an onset of false representations but has assembled the Self to an authentic position of actuality in reconstruction of the economic forces that had perpetuated a reduction of necessary contingencies into a platform controlled by contingent necessities that were posited in the spaces where Being would structure the Self in accordance with the natural necessities of a more sustainable existence, i.e., the rivers, the oceans, the forests, the wildlife, etc. would not fall to human hands or to the conceptions of planetary life as only objects for consumption by the most fertile breed of intelligible misanthropic self-identities, trammeling the terrain of natural well-being as though it were designed for self-discovery as a disposable object to the world entire. Such is the mode by which the realism of this ideal is to become sustainable through its natural determinative presentative administrability.

§2.9 *Being Change.*

To change we must *see* the change, *be* the change, *make* the change. Such that we may perceive ourselves as historical cultural objects, we may posit ourselves as the source of change and in possession of the impetus to make the change, and in this way the changes that are made are to the transcendental horizon. Such as we understand ourselves as *teleological* objects, the Self is posited as the source of change and we are in possession of the impetus to make the change, and this way the changes that are made are upon the horizon of nature. Insofar as we perceive the Self as the universal agent of change and a contingent articulation of the particular meaning behind the proposed change, we possess the dialectical movement in the necessity for change and as such the changes that are made are upon the transcendental horizon of nature. Where it is necessary to be the change, one posits the Self as it is in its nature.   Where it is necessary to be contingent to change, one must posit oneself as a transcendental abstraction—conditioned by the customs and the norms of society and what has been proposed within the political economy as the modality to human progress in reality. However, one must not be deceived by this process, for the will of humanity is such that it is both transcendental as it is natural, and we are upon the threshold of an existential awakening that will begin to identify the nature of the Self as only conditioned by its own transcendental barriers. In effect, the will of humanity is such that the becoming of the species is based within the order of nature, as its truth and most uniform position to the universality that has become a global necessity for the realization of the full potential of human progress. We are thus transformed in-and-of-ourselves, and by way of which evolutionary progress holds the title for something that is identical to the reasons why the perceived economic challenges of the past century have led us to a place where we can no longer subsist in the bioeconomy of our age. The positions that the culture takes as posited upon the horizons of truth, justice, and the American way have now been shattered for all time. It will take approximately two centuries to transform the planet to a universal state, such that the currency of the visions that the wealthy have for this planet are not far-fetched and unattainable daydreams perpetuated by an overpopulated Earth that cannot understand the nature of our species or realize their most universalizable goals. We must Be the Change. In order for this to happen the changes must come from within the natural conditions that have connected us to the biosphere, from the core of the transcendental existential Self. Being becomes transfixed upon the horizon of its own sense of unification and community identification. As long as the doubts are all washed away and a sense of security becomes of an atomized, singular existence, we tend to possess the conception of ourselves as safe within the context of our own aspirations and unified personal goals in attainment. Where a vision of the Self as a Being within its own singular transformation becomes unfruitful, happiness occurs. Where a vision for the Self as a Being within its own universal self-identification becomes fruitful, misery occurs. Why should this be the case? Happiness should be a normative condition for universality, not of the very contingent articulation to the Self that despoils the authenticity of subjectivity through conditions imposed upon the Self by false claims made upon universality by the leading factions that have seized reason in order to make changes that only benefited a select stratification of the population that had other plans for society than the "brotherhood of man".[19] What are we? A Self is a self, the being of itself, and of itself it is the being of the other, the sister, the brother, the mother, the child, etc. Who are the others? Are we more concerned with the Self as a Self, or with the conception of others as selves other to us, and in what proportion to ourselves do they hunt and gather more prosperously than we do—why do we fail within a planned economy that has forgotten to posit distributive justice as a natural right in order to remove human suffering? The conception of Self should be natural, authentic, social, ontological, purposive, meaningful, reasonable, substantive. As it should be transformational, thus. The human soul is an entity in-itself. It is posited by nature and of itself—the purity of Being that is collective as it is universal within conception, the reality of its own existence. Where the world sees a natural self as something only to be controlled or judged, it is that the process wherethrough humanity has not realized the truth of evolutionary development resides within the conception of humanity itself. As a Self I am Being. I am this Being. But what am I to others? What am I in the eyes of those for whom judgment is a presupposition that is based in the logic of the historical or cultural conditions that had made them perceive me in this manner? The nature of change is within its Being, in the Being of nature. A transcendental change is an historical or cultural mark that is made by universality and its origins in the universal conception for humanity. Such that generative or determinative causes may be changed throughout evolutionary *nature*—the dialectical positions have been shaped by the historical or cultural marks thus and we make the change. Insofar as the preemptive or presentative causes may be changed by our transcendental nature—from the authentic universality of Being in possession of its reflexive evolutionary development thus, we become the change. That humanity has seen itself change from within the Self—the Self of its own Being and the conception of itself that is identical to itself in nature and transcendental to itself in history and culture—it is the absolute self-concept. Being is thus posited from within its transcendental nature as the former and is also the conception of what is Other to the Self and the Self of its Other. It is, as such, that Being is intersubjective, and objectivated by the Self of itself, a total Being of nature. That Being is interobjective, it is posited as an object to the Other and an object of the Other to itself and subjectivized into itself; and as such is a plural Being of transcendence. Immanence is subjective to change, while transcendence is objective to change. The object of change is to realize an evolutionary horizon of transformation for humanity—to change subjects within themselves one by one, in order to harness and proliferate proportional changes that will effectuate a determinable landscape of actuality that is as meaningful as it is purposive. The universality of nature is within the Being of humanity—we are the conception and the understanding of change; the being of change through the totality of the existence that defines transcendental nature as a phenomenon to the horizon of change. Historic change is the transformation of the transcendental horizon of being into the empirical horizon of our natural becoming. Cultural change is the preservation of our transformative heritage, and the phenomenological horizon of transcendental progress.

Transcendental nature is the subject-object of change and immanent to dialectic, discourse, logos, and rhetoric. It is that we see the change, be the change, make the change—from contingency to necessity, necessity to contingency. Insofar as changes are signified they are understood through the universal object of change; and insofar as they are symbolized they are understood through phenomenological appearance.

Chapter 3

Enlightenment, understood in the widest sense as the advance of thought, has always aimed at liberating human beings from fear and installing them as masters. Yet the wholly enlightened earth is radiant with triumphant calamity. Enlightenment's program was the disenchantment of the world. It wanted to dispel myths, to overthrow fantasy with knowledge.—Horkheimer, Adorno

§3.1 *Representational Correspondence.*

The enlightened world of sense is something that seemed once to be ever so clear and particular to social strata identifying themselves as the universal class.[20] It is these strata that offered the governing signifiers that vowed for equanimity and prosperity for all. Societies were so enthralled with this proposition that it occurred only to public intellectuals and political dignitaries that what had become the calling for so many was the reification of an empty promise that humanity's salvation were never the object of our becoming—we were only vouchsafed in authenticity insofar as the moment of choice were more significant than the actuality of the decision that was being made. So it is that societal compromise sundered the universal into pluralized social nests, where those for whom the conception of Self would be identifiable as actual to us, would also be conceptually adept at reasoning that we were exponents of a manifold identification that made thought and reason both singular and total to human experience.

As for the latter, we are never prone to accept the positions that have been offered as we become of the Self. Through representations that are posited by mind and machine, ontology and techne, this world is one where the naturalization of the *ego* is prior to contemplative activities—while as Beings, we are part of the spiritual promise that humanity had too long ago proposed—nuanced of an affinity for political naivety and institutional avoidance. In order to correct ourselves within the significations made through the objects offered to us through our quotidian rituals and self-conception, the identification to follow is one where we are to become of dialectic, discourse, logos, rhetoric, *and* techne. A human soul is one that is natural in fascination and naturally fascinating—until the dark half of the societal constructs that had entered the psyche through the will of a force of nature (really simply identifiable as the evil that men do), acts upon the logical side of the brain and is mistaken as the nature of the Self—when in fact it is the nature of the *Other*. For this there is no correspondence, only war. As a total eradication of evil upon this planet is not something that one may readily observe through commonplace habitualities, it is only for one to disengage the spiritual uprising in an awakening of the truth of universality posited within its more favoured breeds than the ones driven by a total and complete expulsion of meaning from this Earth. Such as we only have them within our sights as creatures—some of whom are monstrous in proportion to what is reasonable to evolutionary development—the human will becomes a valuable and useful tool by which all necessary scores are to be settled thus. Given this, the use of violence is not something that is here endorsed, but the use of force is at times something necessary to the nature of the Self.[21] Laws governing reality are universal to the nature of the human organism, and primordial being cannot withstand the caprice of those for whom consumption of what is necessary to reality is unbound by any limitations whatsoever. In that nature is the representation—whether what is signified to the Self is something that generates anger or not is not a question of the sanity of the self as subject that has experienced it—it is a question of whether or not subjectivity should be addressed in this manner by those in full possession of an unhinged free-will that destroys the space of representation for those more concerned with scientific discovery and human progress. Yet where does that leave the creative act? In order to propose that we live in the free world, it will first become necessary to observe a few basic historical facts about the being of consciousness. The natural self first realizes itself through its own objective self-representation—that is the mode of self-realization where an object is naturally posited by and for us. What follows is the conception of existence, which is relational and posited in abstraction of what exists upon the horizons of our own contemplative activities. It is by these means that we become a self-concept and begin to project communicative meaning through whatever signs, symbols, representations or languages that we have within the context of our own self-identification. The Self reflects upon its own object and perceives beyond the object, the coordinates of where other such intelligible existences are represented to the conscious mind. It is in this moment that the self begins to correspond with other beings posited upon the field of meaning. Such that thought is prior to language, language is prior to meaning. Signs and symbols may be thought and intrinsically propose meaning to thought. What is represented to the mind, is represented to the Self as it corresponds with its own nature, positing the self-concept through the understanding that composes the meaning of the Self as subject through its own representative self-identification. As the Self identifies itself as itself, it is within conception that the utility of humanity rests within conceptions of Self through the thoughtful meaning that is proposed prior to the self-understanding. It is in this way that the Self becomes a self for itself and for its known self-representation—identifiable as the conception of the representation that imposes meaning upon objects that are represented to the mind. Thus, the object is identifiable through its own signification as an object to the Self, and thereto an object that may be perceived in correspondence with the conception of Self as other to the object that is perceived. Such that this object is within conception and perception thus, it is universal to the ensuing correspondence that is posited by a representational awareness to the reason an objective relation has been posited and meaningful identification has not yet been made through the Self and its object—the signified that has become known to a self as subject and is therethrough the Being of the Other in correspondence.[22]

§3.2 *Relations of Producibility.*

The revisitation of the Self in its being as representative and a meaning of necessity jumps forward thus into how the relations constituted by meaning are realized within a social topology. The latter refers to beings that are, as such, constituted by the rituals and activities upon the field of actuality that are particular to the structured society in which we live and are universal, only insofar as we assemble the conception of the phenomena governing natural existence is concerned. It is in this way that the synthesis of the social with the natural becomes what is called the socio-natural world. The socio-natural Being is one that is conceived as purposive, meaningful and reproducible. The irreducibility of the former to an axiology of the Self is bound to a position in actuality as concrete, negative, and abstract. From its natural horizons, the Self as subject finds itself within a concrete universality as is given by the immediacy of the Self and is objectively posited by nature thus. The negative condition to subjectivity occurs where the self-concept is in realization of its own self-identification and encounters itself in the opponent, operating as the negative condition to the proposition of universality within its own self-same particularization. Through dialectical positions alone, it is not enough to sustain the positions in opposition to the Other upon the field of actuality. As such all forms of communicative activity within the grasp of a self as subject become tools providing argumentative substantiation for claims that must be rendered, such that the particularity of the Other is sundered to the actuality of the universality represented through universal self-identification. This is the means by which actualities are sustainable to the ontological field wherethrough the coordinates of relations of producibility are made fruitful and evolutionary to onto-genetic transformation.[23] Where relations are producible they are both actual and meaningful. That they are reproducible through the feasibility of the means of production, becomes of an historical tale that is well-known enough to remain outside the present discourse but yet they are so as to be generated by the signifiers that propose a meaningful connection to the sources of nature and society; providing a platform of stability for the necessary accumulation of scientific discovery, so as to propel the planet upon a more favourable trajectory than we have been on for the last five decades, no less. Where we will be in fifty years depends upon the choices that we make in the here and now; and what is approaching is irrevocably daunting *vis-à-vis* the conditions imposed upon humanity, through the genesis of its own self-concepts by those willing to despoil the assemblage of meaningful enterprise into a form that is fortuitous in keeping with the departure from traditional industry culture— into other areas where the propositions that are made are in reality *post-industrial* ones, given the historical conception we now have of industry as a destructive power over developmental human transformability.

The horizons of producibility are based upon both natural and social relations. As the Self is itself as subject, in a concept of-and-to-itself and relating to other such subjects, the relations of producibility are natural ones and in this way objects may become reproducible. That the Self as social Being is a concept of-and-in-another, the relations of producibility are transcendental ones in ontological correspondence.[24] The universal concretion of Being is positional to the Self as the Self of the natural horizon—whereupon its authentic universality is reflexively abstracted *a priori*. This is the purposiveness of the Self before there are any reflexive conflicts that sunder the Self into its own particularization in nullity—whereupon the self-concept wills, once in abstraction of the loss of its own universal self-identification thus. There is an enlightened totality for the brave and the benevolent—willing to risk the mediation of essence, such that universality may once again return to the self-concept. In this way, self-identity discloses itself other intelligible beings within reason, not posited as contingencies but rather within the totality of the Self—a reasonable self of its own actuality. A Self that is the Being of itself—an actuality determinative of the activities that constitute its own universality.

Upon the field of actuality, it is such that Being stands in producible relation to a horizon that is total to the actuality of the self-concept—and there of an ontological awakening that posits the Self within the reality of its own signification as a *reproducible* conceptual identity. The Other realizes itself as other to itself and posits itself as a self-to-the-other, contingent to the actuality of itself yet identical to the self in the nature of Being.

§3.3 *Objects of Thought, objects of sense.*
Existence is replete with objects of thought and objects of sense. The former are objects that are represented to the mind as phenomena or symbols and signs while the latter are things that we can touch, feel, hear, see, smell or taste. Insofar as an object may be thought, it also may be an object of sense and an object of sense may also be represented to thought. Objects represented to thought are represented in our natures and to our faculty of representation. It is thus that they are actual existences, whether real or imagined, and that we recognize them to be things within conception. It is possible to conceive of an object and to posit it, just as it is to become an object for the Self, through one's natural or conditional position respective of the currency of the habitual observations that we might be making through active contemplation. Objects of thought are

phenomenal representations that may be abstracted with conceptions, or be represented to the mind as an actuality of the process whereby reality is presented through liturgical rituals or customs.[25] These objects are identifiable as those belonging to one particular religious practice or another but may also fall into the conception of what are teleological objects—natural objects, spheres posited by the mind *a priori*. Such that the world of objects is out there, it is only natural that some of the former would be represented to the mind and come into conception for the Self, whilst going about daily routines and quotidian practices. Objects such that they are represented to us, may be another Self or the magnitude of a public or private organization that we have recently encountered though; and as such one should be more prone to choose carefully in the activities that one is willing to partake in, such that the objects they have encountered may be too much for the mind to accept into active contemplation. These are of a variety we do not wish represented to us—we must stay away from this or that faction less we are able to identify it as the source of phenomena that has been posited within our minds. Such that objects are also naturally produced by the Self as subject, there may be a biological reason for the experience i.e., hunger, desire, thirst, loneliness, trauma or loss. These objects have often been identified within psychoanalysis as the source of mental illness, but for the present discourse I wish to ponder upon the meaning of these existences—allowing myself full sway in a processual undertaking to identify and categorize whether they stem from what is natural to Being, or from what is historical or cultural in origin. Alas, it is that the objects posited may represent a turn of events acting in liaison with the powers of the opponent; but we are suffused within the grandeur of our own departure downtrodden the path toward the conquering of our fears— lest there be nothing left to chance that the alternative is to utter the word "defeat". I am as one of those that has bore witness to the becoming of my own object, and in the wake of this revelatory distribution of my sense of Self into a phenomenon that were in-itself conceived onto-genetically through ontological praxis, resolves to only demand emancipation where there is no space from which things may be wed to my own personal hubris thus. Reason herself has been willing to accept the objects as representations and presentations of the differences that exist between us— articulated from their genesis in universality—where they present as either men or gods leaves something to be said for the existence of kings, as once it were thought that the existence of them would be productive to humankind in good measure; notwithstanding utter revolt from the peasantry. Objects are things as they are in conceptual abstraction, noetico-noematic observation, self-positing retentive capacitation, phantasy and memory. We know from Brentano and Husserl that objects of nature are represented to the mind as psychological events—even so, it is not that they are events so much as captured experiences that are iterated through our own retentive memory. Most would find the mastery of these sorts of objects to be more possible than the magnitudes of a certain transnational conglomerate; and for this reason providing the mind with enough visual stimulation becomes remedial to the Self—as Being should not be locked in a dark closet for the duration lest the demons begin to appear—consuming each ounce of human vitality until the mind has completely been overthrown. Thus it is never to occur in our meditative conceptions, reading or creative expression, or within the logic of the social transformation that positions the objects as those that fall within the ordinance of needs, rather than narcissistic over-consumption of the others. Where we begin to see what we know and understand, we begin to perceive the possibility of the conception of something that is upon the horizon of our own contemplative actuality. Reality is both the conception of something that exists, and the spatial and temporal coordinates where it is a *de facto* object that we may willfully posit within ourselves.[26] These are the daring objects of the logical world of Rudolf Carnap no less, yet it will be necessary for us to hold on to the metaphysical dimension a little longer, such that we may fully grasp the object as it is in its entirety. In this way it is both an object of thought, and object of sense, in other words a physical object. The latter may be justly signified to the mind through its signifying function and through the optical sensibility appear to the mind as a real thing, as such. In its context it is within justification an existing thing, though we have no particular coordinates, as its appearance is one that is particular to the coordinates of its universalization as an object. It is this that enables us to think of an object or to abstract and perceive it thus—and from there realize its full potential in modal relation to the conception of a second object that may be the owner or possessor of something that constitutes personal property. It is in this way that we have transcended the representative meaning of personal property, leaving nothing out of the imagination than the actuality of the price tag. As such objects of thought are also sensible ones—we think them and may wish to acquire them. They are purposive objects, meaningful objects, useful objects, societal objects and objects of the culture and the arts.

That objects of sense may be thought, objects of thought may be sensed. It is in this way that they are brought into our conception and become the things as experienced as an object to the sensibility, and something that is otherwise represented as a real object that is complete inside our heads—rather than something that has been disassembled. The wholeness of objects is that they subsist in our conception, though they may be divided into their constituent parts. Of this wholeness in reality, objects of thought that are subjects may also be divided into their constituent parts or "cut up" as it were—separated from the properties that constitute *Being*. Lo, how we must heal ourselves of these despots excluding us from our properties with such aggression and ill-will! They shout a resounding "Never!" upon the world stage, where the neutralization of our authenticated existence is to become a reality in the times. Is it thus that we are those that must concede that we "fell for it", or "lost", or is it that there were a bigger picture, portraying the tales of one for whom savage behaviour was not within conception in the throws of an adulterated reification lain bare by a most vituperous passion? Yet it is that the natural objects of Being have metaphysically obfuscated the objects of sense there within conception—we might yet abandon the project of metaphysics such that property is not something outside of our conception. Far be it from me to present the world with an option that gathers the spiritual in the wake of the physical—given that both are purposive to necessity, meaningful, and useful to some; though having fallen asunder the conception of something useful is outside of the act of metaphysical evaluation for the age in which we live. It is, though, that objects to the Self for the contemplative purposes within reason are what interest us—albeit upon actual metaphysical coordinates if we may be so bold as to apprehend them. How are these things to appear to us? It is not that we would falter in conception, nor that we would leave it alone such that reason had no purpose for us in the existence of reality. By these very means, ontology is in the act of investigating and coming to know and understand if ever we are to comprehend these existences as sometimes unhindered by nature governing laws. Why must we accept what is sometimes so difficult to incorporate into the rational thinking

Self—such that our own identification is lost to immeasurable diachrony and past mistakes rather than gaze onward toward the very horizon of our own transformational avolition? It is for this very reason that we make a distinction between natural objects and historical objects, and thus make no allowable synthesis within the object itself possible for the conception of what has been posited by transcendental nature. In this sense, it is only that the objects that are natural are in synthesis with those that are societal—such that the historical sense through which we understand ourselves is an object of the understanding, rather than one that is of an unbridled aggression rendering the Self a mere spectre to its own contemporary self-identification. Societal objects are those for which some will trade-in the former, just to ensure a proper place in the afterlife of financial stabilization. The objects of culture and the arts are many and the entirety of the following several passages should be devoted to them. The ones I will concern myself with are books, paintings, sculpture, architecture, music, film, dance and cuisine.

What they all have in common is form and content, signifier and signified, space and time, purpose and meaning, pleasure or displeasure i.e. appeal or scorn. As the written word posits an idea, not only are the books themselves *objects*, but every word signifies something that may be *objectivized* in thought or an object itself. Greek, Latin, German, French, English interpreted in such a manner as to assign different meaning to how an object is represented in thought for our purposes is the ontological description of language, in that they are all hermeneutically object-driven languages. The proposed subject is not yet the subject by way of a word, until it has been objectivized and become real to the reader—as such language becomes a form of communication that is object-based; rather than being centered upon the subject alone. With this being the case, we read books and become of what they represent—the only real subjects within conception are the protagonists, antagonists, agonists, and miscellaneous other characterizations representing the imagination of the author. In this way the book is a signified and the author is the signifier in the form of which all internal representations in a text, poem or novel are significatory to the inner world that constitutes the Self in its nature. A book is an object of universality in conception, purpose in representation, history in signification, desire in objectification, actuality in imagination,

imagination in realization, knowledge in acquisition—a horizon for future generations. Books are the reason for reason, the meaning of interpretation, existence in necessitation, essence in reformation, a world in valuation.

Excellent companions to books are paintings. Form and colour, temporal space, representation of the object or objects within the frame— beauty and despair, the authenticity of passion, the exuberance and excitement of grandiose expressions to a world entire, the overarching and the remote, the simulacrum and the simulation, the domination and the reverie, the submission and the quiescence. Existence as we would have it realized through the object, its purpose and its meaning. As is sculpture— corporeality and extension, gestural formalization, motion and stasis, angularity in conception, resilience and resignation, composition and authentication. These three cultural forms breathe life into architecture, music, film and dance. The former, while being a reality that conditions or procreates in the act of each of our ontological conceptions, responds to sculpture in a macro dialectic of astonishing proportions. The Spaces where life is experienced offer horizons upon which all contemplative self-actualization posits Being. As in music and dance, architecture is ethereal or concrete, proportionate or disproportionate, meaningful and practical, purposive and expository to human passions. Film is a synthesis of motion through space, picture and sound, density of matter and texture, narrative and dialogue—sensibility and sensation, concept and representation. Dance is the expression of form through content, gesture through purpose, and meaning through time. Cuisine reveals the senses of touch, taste, smell, sight, and sound measurable to the softness, hardness, temperature, components and sensuousness of the dish. It is flavour in conception, desire in confession, dreams in realization, beauty in transformation. It contributes to purpose and meaningful self-expression.

§3.4 *Intersubjectivity of objects in-exchange.*
Such that in the preceding we discussed the senses of taste, touch, feel, smell, sight and sound, it is that these senses may be observed or experienced non-locally or, in other words, exchanged between subjects within the universality of the genus *proximativa*. Objects, as experienced, are transferred from one locus to the next; and their corresponding sensations may also be experienced intersubjectively, as such. These sensations are in the effects of memory. So if someone is eating apple pie,

I may smell the pie, taste it, feel it as though it is in my mouth, even see the pie in my mind or hear the chewing noises as though they were taking place in my own head. Albeit as an exaggeration, since we know from science that most will only have one sensory experience at a time non-locally. Sensory objects are transferred in consciousness and we are able to identify the fact that there is something co-unary between poles of *Being* that posits the awareness of a sensory experience, psychophysically transmitting it through space and time—or here in temporal space. The other senses are also identifiable as these which may be experienced on either pole of consciousness, the noetic pole or the noematic, constituting the conception of a noetico-noematic experience as in transcendental phenomenology—these which carry with them sensory experiences to those that have been particularized in transcendental reduction through a mundanization of the ego, or *ego-object*. That visual, oral, tactile, auditory, or sensuous content are also transmissible in this way, as in transcendental phenomenology, the natural objects of others may be posited for us, and lodge within us a tremendous distaste for certain phenotypes beneath the rubric of our ever-so-disparate discourse and actuality in contemplation. Though that we may see them, hear them, to feel them is never to understand how in fact genuine relations may become unacceptable under such conditions as we endeavor to become adept at realizing the authenticity of our expectations—*ergo*, the constitutive loss to the substance of Being becomes a familiar context within which no such acceptance of this as a formality to realism would become in the least way possible within reason. In this case, the transference of content from one phenotype to another is responsible for a constitutive lack, it is that the relationship must be dissolved; yet where it is simply within the modality of a convergence of immanence with transcendence, perhaps the other should be absolved of the misdemeanor that they have undertaken to pursue. Such as it is, nature governing laws will not necessarily intercept or intervene in the event that a foul has occurred to the transcendental subject that is experiencing non-local sensory experience. Yet does this objectivation of Self as a matter bearing entity posit itself in other minds? Well, indeed it does, as the eclipse of subjectivity by its objectivation thus renders its way into objects that are in-exchange—as these which are in actualized subjects that have transmissible magnitudes of the Self that are self-sustaining only insofar as they *are* exchanged intersubjectively. Such that the will of one phenotype will appropriate the conditions posited by one subject, so must a Self never falter in the reduction by reconstituting and activating their conscious endeavors.

§3.5 *Interobjectivity of subjects in-exchange.*
The object of self or Self-object, is exchanged thus interobjectively. In this way there is an exchange between subjects that is particular to the object of the self as made so by its own subjectivity. Thus a Self as subject posits its own object and it is transmissible in exchange with the formerly intersubjective Being. The determinations actual to one subject may become so to another through the exchange of their conferring objects reflexively. So it is that one subject may experience the determining factors that define another and the other the Self—thus exposing one to the question: What is the *de facto* nature of one subject or the other if this exchange is consistently underway? In order to resist any further diremption of what perturbs me here, I will enter into the matter further by suggesting that one's nature is precisely this. The human genome possesses a necessary biological response mechanism that is self-generating, and is posited by a desire, a need, a request, or a yearning for something that is not present within the Self. Without getting too Freudian on this matter, it is that the Self desires precisely what is in the other that they do not possess within themselves or a property that may authentically belong to them *a priori*. Such as it is, we search for this and gain only insofar as it becomes acceptable to us to persevere in our own affairs in order to exchange meaningful objects that have a place not only in our own proprietary world, but the one that is universal to the totality of the world as an unconditioned whole. Such as it is, this is the modal relation, and allows one to value the Other in their own selfhood—should an expansion of purposiveness become of the universality of the Self as subject. So the objects in-exchange are these which matter to us most, allowing for the future to represent itself to us upon the horizon where we are, in effect, the products of own reproducibility. Within this reproduction, we are both the positing Self of essence, and the essential Self of a posited essence that is for us. By these very means alone, the Self is interobjective and natural due to the abstraction of something that was not particular to their universality and were perceived through a lacking—therefrom reconstituted into an actuality finding its wholeness in completion. We are complete once the

natural essence of the Self has been fully reconstituted in this way and become of the very transmissibility or non-locality of concurring essences situated within a restricted universality. The empirical horizon produces the natural objects particular to the universality of nature governing us as objects in-exchange. We are both producible and reproduced in-exchange and in valuational correspondence with one another—the teleological purposiveness of the means and the transcendentality of the end. What is justificatory to the Being of nature is its transformability and the immanence by which the exchange of values may constitute reality in such a manner as to propose a universality that is more than natural to just one particularized stratification of the planetary substance. It is such that we become the objects of exchange and the subjects exchanging values— entering into modal relations toward the establishment of a future set of goals that are natural to humanity; and reality to the universality that we might propose. It is this that drives us forward toward the horizons of an environmental change that will coordinate an ethical becoming of possibilities in-exchange, and an exchange in possibilities. The moment we become through the nature of the Self, we are absolute of a nature that must be repaired from within ourselves—an actuality that is the reality of the irrevocable purposiveness to the meaning of a clean and controlled sense of Self that is composed of the universality of its own self-determinability. Such that the meaning of this purpose is the reality of Beings-in-exchange, it is also that the objects are these which are composites of the universality of genus that is natural to the restoration of the Self as the phenomena to its own existential noemata. These are the existences that are also transmutable to the Self as subjective, throughout the experiences that resolve to particularizations of the psyche as the form to which its contents must become justificatory in adequation to the transcendental objectivation that had posited the realization of the Self as in-itself—subjective to its own transformation thus. With this the existentialist principle mediating universality is unhindered by the naturalization of the self upon the horizons of its limitable actualization. The exponents to the natural world are such that the psyche identifies itself within the context of its own limitability—becoming the soul of its actualization, and a resource from which the actuality is uncompromised by its sundering into the component parts constituting itself in wholeness. The completion to the Self is realizable through an adequation of its limitability, through which the psyche as ego-object—becoming in the reality of its own expectations—is the Being of its limitable actualization as the sole property of the posited Self that is noematic in composition; while becoming of the natural horizon as the purposive being within the universalization of its own particular transmutation that has gathered the psyche into localized components that have been understood through contingent articulations to others upon the same field of actuality.[27] Such that the progenitors of actual conduct congregate within one particular universality, forgiveness to the exposition of the nature of any given phenotype becomes the necessary adjudication of what the threshold of toleration must in effect become. Such is the relational modality of the Being-of-Self. Insofar as this is an essentialist conception, the nature-self must be seen as real to the psyche that it propounds to gather exponents to a concretion of universality never confounding sensibility within the conception of what is real to the human understanding.

§3.6 *Nature and the objective world.*
The latter, to which the two features of nature and world are identifiable within self-consciousness as objects—the first the being of the nature-self, which is a Self of immanence that has for it a transcendental episteme, is the conception of self as within itself the universality of Self that is posited in contingency as Other *to* the Self. The nature-self is, as such, the self that is posited in singularity, yet is sundered inward toward the horizon of an objective world that is idealist in conception. The objectivation of the self-as-other to the Self is its episteme, the episteme of transcendental nature and constitutes the conception of Being as the self of its other—the nature-self. Nature's governing laws posit the conditions to the Self from the horizons where administrable proprietary aims become particular to the universality of nature and the coordinates through which the Self is identifiable as a spiritualization of its conception through nature as the real of itself and the positions from which identities are posited thus. The conditions within subjectivity have not yet opened to the possibility of image consciousness hereto, yet these provide the basis from which the nature-self realizes its own incarnation through the judgments imposed upon subjectivity by those other to the self. In judgment the Self realizes its own problematic, reconstituting its affairs so as to return to the modality of co-presence and ethereal consciousness of the image—a position from

which the appearances that are also contingent to the transcendental self will deliver subjectivity toward the horizons of the objective world, posited in concert with the nature-self and the transcendentalism of its univocity and transpositional contextualization. Things in this manner are so where Being has realized the authenticity of its purposiveness, and the flourishing of its intrepid sojourn into the elements of nature as a seeker to the truth of its universality and objectivated reflexive self-actualization. So it is that the transmutability of the Self is posited upon the horizon of judgment—yet is still co-unary to the world as the natural object to the Self—thus the world consciousness determinative of the transcendental dominion to Being that is its representative selfness that is total to existence. The nature-self is total to existence only insofar as the self of nature is existence in its totality; yet singular in purpose and whole in its completeness, apportioned to a co-presence of natural objectivation and world-consciousness. It is within this reasoned modality that the Self discovers the peace of itself and the singular totality of the universal void through which the nature-self understands the ethical form through which the content of the Self is to become of the transcendental understanding. The purposiveness of Being is universal to the vision of itself and for this reason alone provides a landscape upon which the symbolic context wherethrough the image is to be posited in co-presence becomes of the transference of content from one perceptual reality to the other—insofar as the understanding discovers the intelligibility of the context therefrom; and recovers the image from a formal abstraction that discloses Being to existence and the objective world to being, as an ideal totality of unified possibilities. Reason is posited by the mind of the vertical understanding, and images of objects of the world are appearances that may be conceived and abstracted from the coordinates where the judgments had been posited through the universality of the subject. What is rendered by self-consciousness thus, is the universality of an objective world in its conception through the subject, identifiable as the author of the idealism that had reproduced planetary wonders within the actualities of the conception of the beautiful or the sublime; rather than the horrors and the pain. Nature in conception may be reproduced in such a way as to illumine the psyche to its intelligible totality upon particular coordinates posited by memory i.e.—regions that one has seen in person once upon a time—they are also the coordinates reproduced through the organic components that are transmissibly generative through the elements and may be perceived as transcendental *noemata*. These are signs to the nature-self, abstractions of possible localities acting as actual referents to the spaces where nature's organisms may be restored through the ethical transformation of the planet—more concerned with what we do to the habitat of millions of species upon Earth. The objective world of nature is thus a representation of the planet in its ideal form to a conditioned self-consciousness, just as it is the temporal existence identifiable as a habitat that must necessarily be preserved—both for the preservation of its own creations, but that the natural existence of humanity will certainly perish also—should we fail to consider the immediacy of our relationship to the elements constituting the universality of the wholeness that constitutes our Being. The evolutionary praxis underscoring an evaluation of the purpose of humanity, is herewith disclosed as this which is biased toward the preservation of the species and the planetary dwelling, whereupon we discover ourselves as collectives and individuated self-representing natural selves, overcoming the departure that we have to make toward the horizons of our own self-preservation through the preservation of nature. It is this co-existence that allots us with the necessary context whereby we become of a naturalistic ontology, more responsible to the environment and less consumptive of the energy that exists upon Earth. It is in this way we that become a species motivated by the authentication of our own ethical transformation that we endeavor to reside within the promise of a meaning to this existence propelled by the appearances of what is possible the purposive unification of the objects that compel us to act—and to project upon the horizon the possibilities of our own transmutability in the quest never to dominate, but to provide for the necessities that are real at the global level. It is within this proposition that the existence of our natures will be able to provide for itself, the nature-self, an authentication of the purposive meaning that is the meaning within purpose itself—a natural science that will revolutionize the way in which human experience transcends the boundaries of the immanence of its own destruction, through the destruction inhering of the transcendental subjects' own understanding. A moment of the past birthing toward its future. That this is the future present by way of the past, where Being is in full realization of its potential as a representation that is signified of and through its very actions—we are the thrust forward beyond, projected upon the symbolization of the existences that are natural to this ontology. That a natural ontology of the world is possible, such that we define this existence as living in the world of nature. It is thus that that we begin to identify our excursions out into the organic unification of Being with its natural habitat—only to discover the constitution of our affairs is identifiably cast out by its own actions. The signifiers that temporally determine the purposes of this existence are these from which the Self is condemned through the vitriol of its others, rather than appointed master within the adjudication of what the entitlements of existential responsibility are. The path that has been chosen by the industries of the objective world are these from which the comforts of jurisprudence and professional acquisition may be enticing, but lest we forget, the damages incurred to this planet are objectively hazardous to the health and well-being of billions of planetary citizens. Inasmuch we must resist the urge to wield power and authority over the landscapes of the field of actuality, the perpetrators of the inhumanity thrown upon our Being is precisely the cause for the outcomes to their own existence. As it is, the wholeness that is posited within the completion of a segmented and fragmented universe brings one to the conclusion that the object of the lifeworld is to recreate a symbolic universe of the transcendental ego, if only to reinstate the ideals that had been posited before the onset of most of the destruction of the twentieth century onward. It is in this way that we will be capable of diagnosing what went wrong and come-up with better strategies to perceive the objects of the world such as they are—such as we would wish for a universe of humanitarian projections of what propels the science of our ways forward within a universality of the reality of the causes, and effectual remedial measures to pursue—such that we preside as voices of reason within a functionalism of the purposes that posit a horizon of truth to Being. Where the immediacy of what is generative of the hegemony that structures the sense of Self as a Being that must be disciplined within an indeterminable solitary existence, the problematic of society and the objective world is within the natural Self as its own positional reality, for which the resolution is conceivable.

Chapter 4

There is indeed present in intuition an ideal activity, having as its object the intuitant, an equally ideal activity involved in the preceding intuition; here, therefore, the intuitant activity is an act of the second order, i.e., a purposive, albeit unconsciously purposive one.   That which remains of this intuition in consciousness will thus indeed appear as purposive, but not as a product purposively brought forth. Such a product is organization, in its whole extent.

—Schelling

§4.1 *Substance, ego, a holistic natural ontology of the Self.*

The facts are the facts, as some propose, yet each of us observes reality behind our own lens and the conception of what is absolute becomes relevant to the notion of what constitutes the Self as both a natural Self, and an albeit quite unnatural and decentered self that only responds to the will of the Other.[28] Whether unconsciously or contingently, we strive to attain a sense of Self that is universal to the modality of our own expectations. Insofar as we produce ourselves as Beings, we do so while remaining in full contact with the conception of what is absolute to the very conception of our own natures, and resolute in the process of projecting purposively with an intentionality toward the object of our desires. That this is, in effect, the very thing that gives us purposiveness to begin with, we become the agents of our own disillusionment—such that the understanding of the contingencies particular to our own sensibility are destructive of the intentionality of our wares. The Self as substance is the substance of the objective Self—the driven purposive Self, intentional toward its other. Whether signified through an unconscious valuation of the Self or not, it nonetheless leaves little room for the phenomena which the natural Self has in reflection, if only to become ever-too-keen to enter into a holistic world of a universalistic valuation of nature, as an environment of change that changes us, and that is requisite of the human intelligence such that the evolutionary process not only has ontological implications for humanity, but offers a completeness to Being that is otherwise absent the reason that compels a futurization of the conditions structuring the enterprises that instantiated an ethical mobilization of acts that will restore the natural evolution of humanity toward a horizon where the products of developmental actualization on Earth will be *post-industrial* in fifty years—such that the actualities of the age in which we live are only scratching the surface of what must be accomplished to protect our habitat, while resurrecting the meaning of this existence to restore the purposes that would lead us closer to rationality, and further away from irrationality. The enlightenment was the period giving us the tools to diagnose the problematics of the day, and we must take full advantage of them. Within the perils of the prognostication that a certain cultural spiritual awakening has occurred upon the planet that is destructive to the project of the preservation of our species, we must thrust through the ambush of the flagrant assault upon what might be pure to human nature, and not an affliction that is cast out into the world with a fury that is beyond tolerability or the sense of a necessary accommodation of plurality, etc. We must gaze into the abyss that had been created by our own mistakes and vow to repair the damages that have been done. Through an understanding of our own natures, we will come to realize the substance of our being is precisely what is produced through the actualities of the existence of our own egos.[29]

Once a transcendental natural Self has posited itself in identity—symbolized to the Other and within the Self as within the Other—the Self as subject begins to realize the truth of itself through ego-identification; which is experienced either as a contingent phenomenon or a proximal actuality to the reflecting self-consciousness. Through this process, ego-identity posits the Self as its truth, and the truth of its other is expressed through the contingency of its own actuality, which bonds the Self within an abstract limitability. Such that it is established in modal relation that the Self is natural to the projection of the contingent other from its conscious sense of self-awareness, *Being* becomes contingent to itself and understands the content of its representations thus, reflecting upon its object and restoring what is transcendental to the self, through what has become symbolic to consciousness. In this sense, the mind is both conscious and unconsciously apprehending the objects of its own contemplation—ontologically apportioned to two realities—one that is revolutionary to human creativity and production, the other that curtails the essence of Being, such that purposiveness has been deposed as the actuality of the self as subject. Ego-identification is the purity of reflexive contemplation, while self-identification is the presentational process whereby Being establishes the context for all of its activities and composes the Self as a natural Being that is willing to restore the spaces of its own proximal dwelling to their most natural state. Inasmuch as the conflicts awaiting the natural Self are real, they are diagnosable and controllable through what is changeable to the nature of the Other, just as it is to the indwelling spaces and environments where actuality becomes a reality in principle, not simply a business proposition that has gone off the rails. Such that the positions of the natural self must be dialectical and the reasoning that accompanies Being must be abstract, ego transference poses a problem for self-identification in pursuit of the naturalization of ego-identity. Does the substance of the natural self possess the qualities that are universal to genus, or is it that the particular reification of the objective self creates a space where the understanding is posited through the contingency of the Other? Where we return to the Self, it is that the natural Self is of this universality, yet it is also that ego-identification becomes contingent—a master signifier becomes determinative of the effectual essence to the natural Self. With this the object of desire is a little more perplexing, since it is such that the needs of the subject must be reasonable dictates to the Self—where we are reflexively posited between Self as subject and subject as Self. In this environment of the Self, it is that the object is of the not-self, as such. Insofar as this is the case we identify it as altogether contingent or unconscious. Being is the Being of itself through and by the Self, and in its nature, natural to itself—hence human nature may also be contingent, though for our purposes, it is to maintain self-consciousness as an accurate measure of both the necessary and the contingent, the conscious and the unconscious.[30]

With this the purposiveness of existence remains within the Self in modal relation, while the universality of genus of the understanding is its conceptual actualization through a holistic enterprise. It is so insofar as reason is the actuality of Being and the actuality of Being is within reason particular to the understanding of the Self. The natural properties of substance that are instantiated as conscious drives are experienced through somatic effects reflexive to the object that has constituted the contingent articulation of ego-identity. To suggest that this is the Self and not its opposite may be to sacrifice reification of content, but nonetheless we must observe the dialectical responses that we have within the universality of our natural self, such that we may attain the authenticity that is desirable to the constitution of Being. To suggest that this experience is natural and we must thus simply reify the content as our own, is an essentialist proposition; and as it has already been observed that the historical and cultural objects are synthesized with the natural object, it brings me to conclude that this is not an authentic Self, as such—as it is synthetic and not a naturalization of the transcendental ego. But where do we go from here, since the pleasure principle is after all essentialist in principle? It is however, that the analytic Self is identical to itself in nature, in both necessity as in contingency—yet that purposiveness is the meaning of our own existence, so to naturalize the unconscious contingencies is to gravitate away from the desire that we have not to become *of* our own object, but to turn this object into *ourselves* through the actuality of choice.

Given this, it is that a transcendental natural Self is providential to the understanding, in that there is within proposition the principle of enlightenment as to the knowledge of Being as the truthful progenitor of the horizon of its own sensible instauration of a meaningful existence. The latter must be singular in purpose, never the result of mass-enterprise.[31] The idealism of our wares is to posit a Self that is not a Being that had been generated purely by commercial desires. Those are the opponents of the natural Self. Such that transcendentalism is both a profound understanding and symbolization of what is representatively signified to human consciousness, it becomes necessary to avoid the commercialization of the Self in order to become transcendental in nature. While relations of production posit the universality of currency as the sole purpose and aim of this existence, it is not for the ones for whom currency loses its sheen, once we realize that it does not provide Being with its own purpose—it merely provides being with the purposes of the Other in exchange. With this being the case, we must move ahead thus, toward the horizon of our own transcendental nature. The reality of experience, is that it is the transformation of existence into concretions of Being—it is thus that the soul of humanity lies within the judgments proposed as adjudications of the wilderness wherein the proprietors of the planetary substance are indwelling features to the architectonic environment we would wish to call our own private sphere of actuality. The public atmosphere today is such that there is no room for ego-transformation, we are this from which the conceptions of Self are truths that must be reckoned with through the standardization of the edificial landscapes of the spaces where reason sits on level ground. As we provide for ourselves, the substance of our actuality is holistic insofar as it is particular to the universality of the rectitude of what proports to establish a sense of conference with the prudential avails of the Other. The rationale behind experience as an ordered possession of coordinates of metaphysical actuality, has to abandon the very conception of the latter—such that we begin to realize that these propose a mathematization of nature—the conception of an intelligible form to which space and time may be realized through precise geometric calculations; those which become integral to ego-formation prior to self-identification. That the organic unity that is principled in the composition of natural lifeforms to a human ecology, we endeavor the realize a uniformity in ourselves as real existences that are natural and posited through the substances of the environmental conditions of our embodiment. The teleological relationship that is posited by ego is such that it is both natural as it is societal. The intelligibility of the human artifice is such that existence is the reality of Being as the reality of its own holistically natural endowment of essence and proprietary substance, proposing a transcendental dimension to reason itself. This is experienced through the representations that are both mathematizations of the natural habitat within the essential substance of the ego, just as they are societal through the particularization of modal relations. As the latter are not universal to the horizon of actuality, it becomes necessary through a holistic natural ontology to elucidate positions identifiable to the causes that form the stratification of significatory activity disavowed by the universality of genus—proportionate to the purposive meaning that is residential in accompaniment and quite unnatural to the habitat of unconscious drives that motivate purpose with an object that posits conditions upon the subject—previously identified as conditions that were not authentic positions from the Being of Self as would fulfill what is transcendentally required at the representational level—toward the formalization of adequate judgments that were propositional to the universality of the unconditioned thus.[32]   As Being is integral to humanity, nature is also integral to Being and the composite of the two sunders the Self of the whole to its parts—not the positing of a Self that is incomplete, yet processual in service of the necessities that constitute the transcendental horizon as a horizon of actuality that has been formed by the natural constitution that has been apprehended in concert with the restoration of consciousness as a neuronal vicissitude that must confer with the Self at the molecular, the atomic, and the sub-atomic level. The Self as subject is such that quantum Being acts in hesitation upon its own proximal coordinates, as the hydrocarbons reproduce phenomena to the subject that are only concomitant to the Self, and not its natural essence. Such that the physical or ontic Self is factual to existence, yet counterfactual in experience, the contingent identification to the Self is particular to the manifold wherethrough divisions of the psyche become realities of the environment in which subjectivity is locked into public utility as the constitution of its modal relativity. The transcendental constitution of nature is such that the Self is not a *de facto* divisional Being, but rather the wholeness and completeness of its naturalistic self-representability.   It is within comprehension that science is a field of actuality where the results are more based upon measurements as evidenced by most of the physics projects that were underway in the twentieth century. Shall we simply agree then that the components of nature are organic composites, while energy systems are ossifications of substances that are clearly dangerous to a human subjectivity of the Self? We reside there within what is principled of the conditions as reifications of the matter-driven potencies that are projections upon a horizon of market-based systems, rather than regress into our caves as though the departure from these human equivocations would be admissible to the exponential influence that physics has had upon *metaphysics*. Nonetheless it leads us somewhere down the road to an adoption of the conception of the term metapsychology.[33]

§4.2 *Self as Echo—somatic extension; psychic intentionality.*

What is metapsychological to the Self is also within its nature, an internal reflexivity to Being through its ontological relation to the Other upon the field of conscious or unconscious actuality. Let us assume for now that it is this which is of self-consciousness, and that we are experiencing others in relation to us as beings we must ground our own objects, resolute that we are identifying a truthful platform of judgment as to how our natures are perceived by others. It is in this way that the other endeavors to conform the Self to what this other would impose upon us, rather than to conform to our own objectivation as self-identical to ourselves in nature as in Being; and in this way become the product of the purposiveness of the Other before realizing our own objectives. Given that the community substance inheres of a subject as Self—through the agency of the others in relation to us—we nonetheless find it unsettling that the uniformity of substance is exclusive the nature of Self that is our being, and thus we resist the causes of the other in order to posit the Self such as it is in its most vital and useful form possible. This phenomenon is what is called the *echo* to the self—the reflexive representative content that is posited upon the field of actuality while we are becoming self-conscious and awakened to the particularization of intersubjective differentia that are inherent the moment of presentative transcendentality. We are here objects *to* the other, insofar as they may posit within our own objectivity as the purposiveness and truth to our own existences, but yet we are not the purpose or the truth of our own existences, as we have not posited this as such from a Self that has been authored by our own natures—we are a Self that has been posited by the wishes of the other, and have become of the Self only insofar as we have allowed the prevailing judgments to belong to a particular class of the citizenry; rather than to the authenticity of our own posited transcendental becoming. It would be thus that the spirit of humanity was within this conception—the notion of what is functional to them must also be functional for us—less we begin to embroil ourselves in any dispute that will transcend the limitations of our time on this Earth. The dialectical position than inheres of the self-determinability that is ideal to the cause of an authenticated productivity is within the potencies of the will to project beyond these echoing boundaries, but need I say more than to propose upon the matter—with the odds cast away, as though there were nothing transformative to acquiescence thus—but by decree of the echoes of an obfuscated and shadowed stratification of those that had first begun to recognize the downtrodden wares of the forbidden from their own exonerated passions, into the dust of the lost years still looming, a waste of forgotten tales revealed. The causes of humanity's resonating signification, bouncing from the walls of each solitary space where time is moving more slowly than it disappears, forsakes even the most weary from the needs in apprehension of a belonging that is transparent only to its own reflection. Human souls are these which are ambushed within the spirituality of their own desires, and the necessities of this life are of this world—yet of another one that has been constructed by our own narcissistic selves. Let us depart this wisdom for another, the echoes of the being that is real to you, to me, to those living within the universality possible to the naturalization of the ego. Where the souls of all are not at peace, there is a restoration upon the horizon that is of a plenitude more favourable to the cognitions of being— the positional residence where the spaces of reflection are never under siege by outside powers with inflammatory judgments and unfounded prejudices and biases. Alas, make the escape—existence must be just, in denial, evil. There is a sense that those that have been more prone to deny the expressions that constitute a human soul are acting in liaison with several of the more destructive forms of evil in existence upon the planet. We must avoid these at all costs. The purposiveness of being is to shelter their natures, such that echoes of the Self are those awaiting such expressions; and the judgments that will propel human authenticity beyond the limitability of its own evolutionary expectations. The substance of an argument is the meaning of the purpose, and the meaning of the purpose is its substance. Humanity's task is to further the species while remaining true to the totality of its environmental coordinates. We are those that are at our best when our aims are universal and our purposes are driven by the conditions of a universality that has been formed by the natures that have not resisted the transformation of the Self, into the vitality of its direction and the thrust of what propels meaning forward—beyond the limitability of the echoes of the Self that we must direct ourselves toward with ego-intentionality.[34]

Somatic extension is understood as the projection of the coordinates of our own psyches to other loci, thus. We are projected beyond the Self, toward the other in extension and relate to them at the ground level as beings that are positional and apportioned to the reality of the Self through its nature; and the reality of the other upon the locus of its own judgment. Such that this constitutes the sense of intersubjective relation factual to experience, the psychic intentionality toward these loci is a purposive duality that stands in property relation between the locus of judgment and the locus of perceptual experience. The symbolization of the Other is particular to a concrete universality—outside of the nature of Self there is no such signification, otherwise it is understood to be one that is delusionary in context—in consideration of synthetic judgments a priori that are universal to the nature of Self. As we have not denied Kant in this way, it becomes a matter of whether or not this is a metaphysics that has been ruined, or whether it is tenable to hold any such things as these within the nature of Self. How is it then that our intentionality toward the Other is not an abstraction of their own natures, and of our own ego naturalization? It will be necessary to examine this through the conception of the determinative causes that were formerly posited. As the nature of Self is now a psyche that is intentional, having undergone ego formation, the projections of being must be real to the actuality that is understood as the authentic existence of the Self, such that it has not simply abstracted from the horizon of actuality a nature that it now begins to call *its* nature. It is in this sense that we understand synthetic judgments a priori, as abstractions—in other words that we would be unable to posit the reality to our own object, such that we have already begun to understand the Other more than ourselves, *before* experience. Within this realm of the understanding, it is that the Self is natural to itself only insofar as it understands the other, and therewith has an understanding of itself *as* the other. But if this were the case, and the other were in the nature of self, it would be a *de facto* self-same representation, which is never the case where we have already become of the nature of Self—that is entirely total to the being of the Self and only of its other in intentionality. This representation of the Self as its *other*, is really of an analytic a priori, in other words—we are bouncing and echoing upon the field of actuality as a being toward its others. It is in this way that the Self is plural in otherness, but must emancipate being in order to realize its most authentic natured state.

§4.3 *Individuation.*
What is determinative to Self as its presentative nature through the others, is not determinative to the Self of its individuation. What the latter does, is expose the Self to the psychic memory through sensory data, involuntary sensations, unconscious drives, and distortions to the authenticity of what in truth constitutes the manifold of human relations in our dialectic. For one to become a natural Self—contained within the self and of the Self—one must stand upon the coordinates of its own modal relations as the aggregate of the wholeness that composes what is natural to being. We are the souls of the many, the spirits awakening to the transmutability of the possibilities of the human understanding—the potential that we have as a species to project beyond the mortal coil of our own reduction into a becoming that is more real than the obfuscation of what has been universally symbolized to the concretion of the existence of the real within us. As Goethe once said: "I am what I am, so take me as I am!". This is the soul of humanity. To be the Self of the Self, the being of itself and stand there upon the coordinates of its own nature to realize the precision of their wares as the actuality of human becoming—what is revolutionary and evolutionary to each upon the thresholds of an imagination that is more grandiose and vast than the horizons of the past. The possibilities of the conception of the Self as natural to its own identity is the reality of this age, the purpose and the meaning that will outlive a present that is condemned to a position that exists only in response to the forerunners of a fledgling economy, seeking a justice that had concealed what were human progressivity in justification. The solitary individuated spirit of its own actuality is an exponent of the reason that the delivery of the mind from its conditional flux—rendered false by the actuality of a failed regime of oligarchs, providential in the wake of their own savoir-faire—is the becoming of individuation's nouvelle regime of the nature governing laws that will to explore outer regions to the psyche, existing upon deeper levels of consciousness so as to render them a voluntary expository of revelations—disclosed to those with a willingness to become of the same naturalization that has underscored the judgments of the illumined and justificatory beings to the universality of what classifies a Self as authentic to its own self-identification, and conditioned only insofar as it has posited itself in modal relation to the realities than had condoned an evolutionary praxis thus. So it is that nature's governing laws are the joie-de-vivre of

the Self, the proximity where truth and justice are never to be condemned to a life of servitude. The epoché of this naturalization is its transcendental hypostatization of nature, existing within Being as a reality constituting its own judgments and conceptions of what are the principles becoming of the objects immanent to the Self as objects of the Self and to the Self in ownership of its individuation, thus.[35] What is exemplary of psychic individuation, however, is the objectless sensory experience to which a Self has no awareness of the conditions of its own actuality; thus it is that individuation be not an exposition of psychopathology, so much as a necessitation as to what is medial to transformation or self-individuation from the sensory experiences that are posited as psychic facts—whereto the objective Self that has become an object for the psychoanalyst, has returned to the subject, and the psychic reality has become the property of the subject once again. It is thus that ego transference precedes the logic of ego-transformation. The analyst and the analysand exchange egos toward the finality of the goal of an evolutionary ego-transformation that instantiates the authentic subjectivity that had first only encountered the Self in a totalization of the phenomena of the others as agents to their own purposive objectives. In this manner the Self was the effect of a systemization of preemptive or presentative causes, pledging to an outcome for the Self that were not of its own volition. It is as such that the Self were influenced to a large degree by communal relations and not the masters of their own destiny. Through an ongoing process of psychic evaluation, the Self returns to its own nature, becoming the transmutability of its own departure from the conditions superposed of the Self by external powers of mediation—not the universality for which the self-identity had yearned. But of this particularity it is that it were composed of the authenticity of a universality that were particular to another stratification to the possibilities of human experience—grounded in historical culture and the purposiveness of the age in which one lived upon the threshold of the twenty-first century. Those that perceived the beauty of this period were often swayed by its radiance and likely unwilling to leave the image-consciousness behind for a departure onto the landscapes of nature's principled and undying affair with the laws of humanity. The wholeness and completeness of Being is the possibility of reason toward the realization of what is identifiable the purposes of this naturalization. Through ego-transformation and an objectivation of the meaning posited by the understanding of what is the reality of our purpose, the human will becomes upon the terrain of its own ideation as the reason and the purpose of the actuality of its own causality. We are the determination and the resolve to thrust past the obfuscation of the universality of our own teleological ends—the authenticity in necessity and the necessary authenticity. The transformative power and the movement of an age when what is perceived is a horizon that is composed of a reason for existence and the existence of reason; a meaning for our purpose and the purpose of our meaning; a justification for our being, and our being in justification.

§4.4 *Pluralization.*

The nature of Self as plural yet whole exists in its own ethical transformability to its most authentic state of being. Plurality is an actuality to the natural Self in its authenticity—identifying the particularizations that have occurred upon the field of actuality. The actuality of the nature-self in plurality is its authentic conditional changeability to the naturalization of its own object.[36] The structure of the Self is its nature-in-authenticity and freedoms are expressed through generative and determinative authenticities. Plurality in conception posits that there *is* such a thing as reality—others represented to the Self as doing something different within a similar conception of universality—the conception of which is the nature within the particular universality that has become presentative to the reflexive effects of the conception of the ego as an object within nature's redemptive transmutability. Inasmuch, nature's governing laws are universal to the pluralization through which the conception of their genus is only exclusive to the de-naturalization of their unchangeable immutability. Such as being is primordial, it is of its objective essence, universal to genus, mediated in its own immediacy, which enlightens the ontological field of actuality—opening it to image conceptions. The objective Self abstracts a conceptual being that has become intelligible to the Self through its own symbolization, and so it is signified as a remote subject. Returning to an individuated state of self-awareness, being becomes in the immediacy of its own existential conceptions—rendering the Self in a conditional flux that posits the object to the Self anew—once again entering the scene upon the landscape of pluralization, where modal relations are activated thus. Such that Being is contextualized through an awareness to its own humanization, the Self retains its purposiveness that has been restored by the telos of human nature.[37] Primordial essence is existential as a transcendental appearance for each Self that is situated within an actuality that may be ontologized into both its symbolic image, as well as its representative nominalization. As such a universality of the Self is posited in singularity, only to confer with the purposiveness of an abstract existential objectivation.   Provided there is a hylozoistic reformation to primordial form, the nature-self projects in immediacy the objectivated empirical conditions upon the locus of judgment, where the Self has been naturalized despite the representational plurality of its position to the field of actuality. The authenticity of Being is posited as its causal nature within the spheres of activity where the Self is transformed from a previous state of individuation, into a visible being of primordial actuality that may be symbolized to Others within individuated pluralities. These are the symbolic spaces where the semiosis of logos activates emancipatory signification of the pluralized beings thus, illuminating consciousness with the spectres of the Others within conceptions that are identical in signification to the symbolic contextualization of subjects in their primordial signification. In this way, the nature-self is the reality of the Self within the volition of their posited conditional awareness of the signification of the Other, within the concrete universality of its own privative conception of plural subjects within the logic of the multitude— held beneath universality of a similar conception thereto, a polyuniversality of sorts. The modality of relations is posited through the conception of Others as individuated selves within a plural network of social actors, posited or projected in representation of a purposiveness that is natural to the common ground posited within an abstract universalism, from which the coordinates to the latter are positions where attribution is acquired within the logic of its own purposive attainability. The Being of Self is its own selfness, the nature of its immanence and perceptuality—the spirit of the relation and the relation of primordial spirits—actuated as positional subjects locked into the purposiveness of a mediated universality, where the Self posits a dialectical position—retracting from presentative causality in order to naturalize a purposiveness that is authentic and conditional to the universality of the Self. The Self is unified in its own nature. Insofar as it is plural, the Others are contingent and identical within the essence of the self. With the unification of individuated self and pluralized self, a total Self is posited. The question here is whether the actualities within the nature of the Self are quintessentially epistemic through activations of a logical techne, or if a synthetic judgment has obfuscated the purposiveness of being; such that the modality of relations is causal to a sense of avoidance concerning responsibilities that are existentially actuated upon the field of actuality, as necessary to the preservation of the actuality of the nature-self.   In its purposiveness, the Self posits the Self toward an attainment of a positional stance whereupon essence is integral to the meaning that accompanies Being, as the totality of observances that are operative necessitations to subjective aims, conditioned by the naturalization of the transcendental subject, such that the purposiveness of being is teleological rather than historical or cultural.   To posit what is necessary to Being in its authentic expression of the totality of purposive meaning, is self-conditioning through an organic unification between body, mind, and spirit.   The mind-body—in the relation that is both natural as it is plural—is not natural in its pluralization, as the causes identifiable as the root purposes of the Self are not within the representations of its Others; they are in effect the transcendental self-identity that is posited in contingency once the Self has observed itself through the *telos* of nature. As these are primordial conditions posited through purposive aims that are biased toward necessities rather than objective desires or wish-fulfillment, the nature of Self is such that its Being must never be solely conditioned through its own pluralization, but is the cause of its own authenticity as the agent of the transformative capacitation of the meaning underlying what is consequential to the positions created by preemptive or presentative causes; which have been conceived through administrable or controlled effects that manufacture the authenticity of the Self within an historical cultural context, thus jeopardizing a more sophisticated resolve to naturalize authenticity as a function of its primordial functionality as unified, plural, and total to being.

§4.5 *Multidimensionality.*
Excursions of the Self are these from which there are a world of objects, conceived within the purposiveness of what has been spiritualized through the accompaniments to the interior space where contemplative actualizations of Being are sundered to positions from where we explore the distances outside the mind, through a dimensional context where language becomes operative to the nature of the world, posited as a field of

actuality thus. Insofar as we are conditioned by our own natures, the causality from which such observances of the wilderness of our inner perceptions becomes an affair with a symbolic reality, the Self is propelled through a logic of abstract necessities positing a state of intersubjective flux. It is such that the dominion of the world of facts is ushered through an assessment of the validity of the latitudes and longitudes of the geometry to the spectres of what may be envisioned, through the awakening of the resources available to the possibilities that are providential to the locality of certain naturalized components awaiting the surveillance of our innermost inquisitive condemnation of unforgiveable conduct. The horizons of signification are such that intelligible objects that are within our purview—such as a museum, an art gallery, a theatre, or a cottage in Switzerland, become of a certain multidimensionality to the remoteness of the acquaintances that are within the grasp of nature's governing laws. The mathematization of the Self into equalized component parts of the whole, resonates across a universe of possibilities that shatter the conventions of the modernity that had vexed post-rationalism beyond its return as the form by which post-modernity could be understood as the immediacy of the radical non-conformists. However, as rationalism is primary to reasoning, the abstract loss that we suffer creates the dialectical impetus to aestheticize our own judgments as the necessary plane of reality where existing dimensions of reality become layered as reflexive objectivations to the psyches that were awarded the explorative behaviours upon the outskirts of their own social imaginary—the angularity of justice reformed, so as to expose what is transmissible to the Self, of the Self, and by the Self, through abstract reasoning and revolutionary contact with the fragmentary beatitude of an augmentation to the composite nature of abstract subjectivity. The total Self is in subordination of this phenomenon, attracting a wilderness of existential supervenience that is bound to the obligations of the structures identifiable as the nature of self in absence of its own primordial self-relation. The dimensions of perception are, as such, composites of symbolic imagery and reflections upon the conceptual targets that penetrate naturalization with the transcendental aesthetic of something projected from a distantiated source that is never to be comprehended or understood. Thus the objects represented to the mind are these from which dimensions of reality that are conceptual, form within the clarity of the resolute abstractions of the dialectical Self—a being for whom reality is never distorted or obfuscated by entities that embody an accidental discharge of human consanguinity—thrusting the Self toward a dissent that is unguarded by the authenticity of its wares. The natural reflexivity of humans is within the actuality their own sensible promulgation of authenticity, as a dimension to possibility that is multiplied through its observational acuities. The multidimensional Self is the natural Self, insofar as the understanding is amplified in abstraction of its horizontal signification as a transmutable objectification of reified authentication.

§4.6 *The Nature-Self, The Nature-world.*

Through the objectivation of what is conditional to humanity, within reason and the purposiveness that is posited by the natural being of Self, the conception of nature is such that it is of the Self, and the conception of the Self is such that it is of nature. What we know from the Self of its nature, we also know of the natural self or the nature-self. In this way the former is posited as real to the human condition and definitive of its encumbrances total to the experience of the Self as a being of nature. The natural environment of this planet provides the necessary conditions for the existence of life forms, and humanity thus articulates its positions within its own organizations i.e., family, civil society, state, world, etc. in contingency to the universality of nature.[38] The twenty-first century's aims at realizing a universality that is closed to particular stratified groups of the population has failed, thus universality in its essence is adulterated by the forms through which we may realize its existential possibilities. As we are closing in on a new age of history, it is of the utmost importance that we thrust forward with a potential definitive of the necessities that are upon us as natural selves—essences that are universally identical to ourselves in nature and thereby the social actors responsible for the outcome of what is happening to the species occupying this world. Such that the essence of humanity is never lost to a particularism that will overrun human progress, we transcend the boundaries of a fragmentary reduction of the purposiveness of being through the dialectical reasoning existing within us as contingent to the universality that belongs to the order of nature. It is in this manner that a more meaningful conception of what is necessary to human becoming is particular to the class that has appropriated the *telos* of nature as the reality to the purposes determinative thereto. In so doing, being becomes of its nature therethrough of an evolutionary praxis that is both natural as it is technological.[39] Insofar as this is the case, we posit the nature-self in communion with the nature-world. Welcoming forward a horizon of the univocity of humankind—a departure from the despairs of the past toward the future of our choosing. We can either choose to begin again—realizing the authenticity of a purposive nature-self—or deny what is posited right before of our eyes—the teleological natural technologization of the lifeworld that we embody, the soul of a population that has not lost to its predecessors, or fallen sway to the evil that men do. The spiritual awakening of our age is upon us, we are the hunters to a wilderness that is preserved, the gatherers of the raison-d'être of our time. The human mind is such that it is a mind encumbered with a reasoned existence, a purpose, self-identity, and a meaningful sense of what has been restored through a return to the elements that had first posited the *techne* of our ways. The world is such that it is a world of nature; the nature-world is the world of self and the nature-self is of itself *world*. The ways of existence that had dominated the previous four centuries have thrust upon humanity the dawning of a horizon less favourable to the outcome that had been suggested by the inherent positions and providential nuances presiding over nature's governing laws, as though the very conditions of this life were cast by the meaning of the experiences that had generated them. The future that is upon us will not only be defined by our actions in the present, but also the approach that we take to the interpretation of what has come before—as causes to the effects that had perpetuated a history from which the transformation of this age would only become possible through a coming of age that were still beyond our grasp; a momentary lapse that had forbidden the arrival of the proprietary aims that would come to determine a universality that were within the conceptions of those for whom the authenticity of our natures, is the liberation of our natures from the freedoms that have cast a dark shadow upon the prosperity of the human organisms occupying Earth. The history of *Being* lies within the shadows of its own undoing, and we the natures that are transcendental to the uniformity of the becoming of what will recondition planetary life, toward a purposiveness that exists in the evaluation of an inexorable order to the necessity for change and the finitude of a darkness that had beset the population—draping a shroud of disrepair—condemned to the losses of the past and the restoration of what will shed new light upon the meaning of what is within the grasp of those for whom what awaits is still within reach—a period where humanity's laws are the currency of its wares—the purposiveness in justification of the possibilities of purpose; and the justification of purposiveness in the purpose of possibilities. A glimpse outside the veil of the memory of a reality belonging to the undoing of meaning, projecting revelations to a universe that is natural to a world that embodies nature just as nature responds in its effects.

The objects of the past are these which hold the memory of our achievements, just as they exist as obstacles in the realization of what the perceived valuation of the present moment of our existence projects. The technological developments that we have seen since the end of the Second World War have posited the social forms that are actualities to the horizons of being existing as totalities, and may threaten the experience of the natural becoming of an evolutionary praxis that is determinative of the modality of authentic relations of producibility.[40] For humanity, the *telos* of nature is the reproducibility of the species, and as such a purposiveness that must not undermine the progress of what the truthful meaning to human experience must become in the years ahead. What is real to us, is that where there is the conception of *us*, it becomes quite identifiable that there oftentimes can be no such thing. The breakdown of societies into stratified communities in determination of the purposes that are beneficial to the latter, presents a problem for the conception of the nature-world as a unified totality in presentification of the proposed universality inhabiting the conception of transcendental nature as an empirical existentiality, allowing the Self as subject to be conditioned both by a sensibility that is governed by ethical choice, just as it is posited within the subject as a truth that is identical to the Self in its nature—reflexive self-identification. Between Self and subject, subject and object, *Being* is expressed as rational, encumbered with reason, self-relation, and relations to the others. As such the nature-self is constituted as an immediacy of the object that is conditioned by the ethical understanding of the Self. The object is the immediacy of the condition to the Self as such, but still the transcendental understanding mediates certain behavioural practices, considered unethical to the essence of modal relations. The Self is the self of itself as this ethical being, the counterpart to the whole that is particular to itself in its own transcendental understanding, yet universal to itself through the nature of what is positional to subjectivity, as it undergoes a reflexive conditioning as a social being; and a Self in existence upon the coordinates of its natural place in the world. So it is that the coordinates to the nature-self constitute being to the nature-world. Yet to state that the latter is a world of nature is to become too much of the existence of nature as the primordial expression of humankind's survival instincts. That necessity would articulate itself in the form of savagery is never to be considered impossible, but the position that is being taken is that a totality of the ethical substance of the planetary organisms as complete to their own proprietary natures, and never reflexive to the judgment of women or men, moreover, posits the natural substance of Earth as the natural substance of Being—a planetary edification of the existence of a species conditioned by the immediacy of its own purposes only where they have become identifiable to the authenticity of the judgments that are posited by reason *a posteriori*. Alas, judgment is ever operative to the nature-self, the modal relations that govern the actuality of our responses, and the nature-world—for the time in which we are living, a concept that is as breathtaking as it is foreboding—that the world is upon the edge of a new age of scientific and technological discovery that is revolutionizing the existence of the human species, and how we perceive ourselves as universal beings. The aim is to become of our natures, that they are what is responsible for the illumination of what propels the disclosures of invention forward through the crises and the desperation of those for whom the abandonment of comprehensible structures to the Self cast them into an abyss of their own undoing and a total absence of logical reasoning. These are not the ills of the nature-self, these are the ills of the order of things that are conditioned by administrable or controlled causes—institutional and transcendental in origin. We must conceive of ourselves as natural beings in order to conceive of ourselves as transcendental beings. We must conceive of ourselves as ethical beings in order to exist in transcendental nature. The essence of what is structural to existence is the existence of what is structural to essence. The wholeness and the completeness of what is Being, is the absence of its totality and its totality in absence—a reality to content that is posited as a truth to the Self that is determinative of the world in which existence is the reality of its purpose.

The horizon upon which all such existences as are real to the human condition, is this that is posited as its truth and the syntactical connection that one has to existence in space and time. As logical beings, the totality of this existence in logic, is its accompanying reason and the reason that is its accompaniment through each choice that is made, and every abstraction that is brought into the reality of the nature-self. That this Self is of the world, nature is of the world and nature is the Self of the world-self—a conditional impossibility for a universality that is one posited by nature's governing laws, thus. Yet, we do not fear the becoming of an age where the reality of humanity is its natural substance; and the sole purpose of our time on Earth is to ameliorate what is conditional to humankind—to posit a truth that is not an abstraction of what has been demonstrated as the real essence of our species. It is thus, that the realities of humanity are not abstractions, these are existences that have coordinates in actuality, and must be ethically engaged through the practices determinative to the authenticity of transcendental nature. It is within this in principle that existences to the real are actual in existence, both diachronic and synchronically represented to the mind through particularizations of Self within the context of a universality of the understanding. Such that they exist in diachrony, they are signifiers to a present horizon of the past identical to the self-in-nature, and such that they exist in synchrony, they are signifiers to a future horizon in the present form of the understanding. In this way the understanding is both diachronic and synchronic to the nature-self. It is in this way that universality in nature is the possibility of universality in the world, and as such a wholeness and completeness that is other to the Being of Self.

The latter as an object to the world is what will be called a world-self. As a sensible being that is symbolically represented to the world, we begin to understand things such as international relations and what were once institutional forms of administrative assembly. With the technological revolution it becomes more possible to have such world figures in perception, and it is for this reason that we identify transcendental causes as preemptive or presentative—such that a dialectical abstraction or positing of a world figure in actuality would be generative of the transcendental *episteme* to the nature-self. Further to our rubric, in order to identify certain world leaders, or to intersubjectively self-represent to them—beyond the controlled effects of our *own* leaders, it becomes a question of prudential judgment and where one sits in the order of things. Such as it is, within the symbolic logic identifying nominal coordinates at the global level, the horizons of actuality are such that this exists not in necessity but in contingency—which is not to completely dismiss the authenticity of the aestheticization of the signifiers within particular universalized spheres of planetary actuality. One must simply narrow down to the target from the universal (nature) to the particular (transcendental) in order to achieve the desired results. That it is, in effect, conditional to human nature to perceive objects of interest and to turn away from objects possessing no value to us, we regain a certain controlled stance toward the manner by which one must approach the aesthetic understanding. Of a nature-world there is a wholeness and completeness to the totality of the natural planetary elements and species, and of the nature-self there is only the totality of *beings*—such that we identify humans as in full possession of self-representability and a comprehensive ethical understanding (which since the technological revolution would deny most subjects).[41]

Gathering what is edificial to the context wherethrough we realize the authenticity of the intelligible realities that are posited through modal relations, we come to the apex of a lost and forgotten allegory of the ways of the world, and why we are here in guidance toward an understanding of what is the most ethical vision for humanity of the spiritual realm—what are the purposes for humans? Are we simply here to identify ourselves or to consume the objects of the world such that we may experience the joys of planetary life without destruction and pain, suffering and loss? It is within us to search for what is identifiable to ourselves as the source of what constitutes a meaningful existence, yet the modality to which this is expressed through Being is what will come to identify us as creatures that will either survive within the cohesion of a necessary historization of this life, or a contingent culturation of what had yet to appear as the most fertile ground that we have for inclusivity and univocity to the human project of evolutionary praxis. That we are neither good nor evil as we are conceived is a matter to be approached in the context of whether these determinations are conditions of society or conditions to nature. I hold that it is the former that has created the aberrations of this world, and that it is never too late to identify the historical processes that developed the world in such as way as to produce a beautiful soul or a ruthless sociopath. Let it be that the understanding of our nature is this which is conditional to the proposition that as we evolve, the souls of humankind will become more at peace than at war; and we may be able to change what is conditional to the political economy in order to starve possibility of the brutality that some have been genetically engineered to purvey. This is a radical form of humanism that will personify our existences as actualities with the capacity to love more than hate, give more than take, listen more than speak, and transform more than degenerate. As an upheaval to the ways of the past, our purpose is to be delivered to an ethical space where the future is upon the coordinates of a horizon where what is real is revealed, and what is false is condemned as the irrationalism of an age that we have only now to surpass.

Notes

Chapter 1

---

[1] As a condition to the Self, it is posited as total to its universal context only insofar as it is identical to its conception in nature. Here I am questioning the authentication of the cogito as an immaterial relation to primordial Being. It is my intention to realize something synthetic between Spinoza and Descartes in order to set the stage for further contemplation on the origins of the natural Self.

[2] Drawing of the distinction between Kant's analytic and synthetic conceptions of experience as *a posteriori*, I am here elucidating a contradistinction between knowledge of the Self through an immediacy that is subjective to Hegel, while positing that the immediate experience of Self is objective and thus exposing the conception of the natural Self first as an objective immediacy—thereby making reflection key to the positing of its nature.

[3] the reality of the former being its actuality, and the object the condition to the universality of the expressions of Self where its own reality is the experience as a naturalized being.

[4] This is utilized in order to posit the conception of the Self as subject and objective to the Self through its identification with other "beings of nature". As such the conception is of being as a reality to the Self; but being only insofar as it is both its objective and subjective nature—positing a condition imposed by the world and one imposed by nature itself.

[5] Here I am providing logical coordinates to nature as the horizon of actuality from where conceptions of the Self become through the universality of genus as though planetary changes also affect the Self in its own understanding of what it is.

[6] A neologism in identification of the dynamics of the logically natural Self within the identification of its binary objectivation.

[7] As known by Kant to be objects of the empirical understanding; the phenomenal representation understood as objects to reason.

[8] Such that the universality of genus is the planetary substance of all living organisms, substance is posited as universal to Being and reified as such through its immediacy of subjectivity with its object, while essence is the actuality of a "Being of Self".

[9] I am essentially establishing a context for Being where the noetic pole (subjective perception) is posited in a teleological unified field of opposites where the being of self is identical to itself in nature.

[10] Such that the teleological end it becomes is given as the primordial substance of existence, there is nothing dialectical between being and nature itself—these exist in the form of representations where judgments do not alter the state of being to the former—rather being subjective through society is dialectical in

nature such that human progress takes the form of real change to historical cultural subjects.

[11] Here there is something both Kanto-Hegelian and Kanto-Husserlian—less I posit something so audacious as a Hegelo-Husserlian phenomenology.

[12] From Early modernism to modernity not only was it a time for the development of societal realities before the industrial age, it was also a time where language was beginning to identify natural human behaviours as identified in the writings of William Shakespeare during the Elizabethan Age. It is also that modernity identifies "man" as "himself"—and as such a man of nature.

[13] Here I am reinforcing the concept of "transcendental nature" as immanent to the Self as subject and determinative of what is both universal and particular to self-identification.

[14] The position taken here is that identifiable logical rectilinear coordinates as in Descartes may be identified, such that a "symbolic imagination" recognizes non-localized images upon determinative actual coordinates from a posteriori knowledge i.e., places that one has physically been at any given time (but also abstractions reasonable to such logical coordinates).

Chapter 2

[15] This is, of course, given that the conception of Self is both natural as it is transcendental—thus of its own transcendental nature. Hegel's conception of intelligible reality as an emptying of the Self is given to the conception of the image content as transcendental or symbolic and determinative to the Self as an intellectualized Being.

[16] Given that the locus of actuality may be symbolically represented through the universality of genus, it is such that these coordinates are only viable where concerns an unmediated actualization of their transcendental signification, thus. It is that the locus of actuality is precisely the point where a signification becomes necessary as a possible contingency through modal relations.

[17] It is thus that the universality of genus as the natural object to the Self is posited as more authentic than its transcendental culturation through modal relations. Such that the latter are realizations of past unverifiable authentications to the Self, they are considered logical to the synthetic coordinates of the locus of judgment, where a more sophisticated naturalized Self articulates the maturity of its own coming of age.

[18] The conception of human nature as having already undergone the transformation into Being that would make ethical changes to the landscape of human endeavor at the planetary level, is an expression of a sensibility governed by the universal context where humanity has been historically bound by its own hegemonic particularizations. In this sense, universality is only possible where the authenticated natural Self is positing a posited from as connection to the biosphere that is already founded upon the principles of a universal actualization

of an ethical planetary project that is in attainment from horizons of actuality beyond the century in which we now live.

[19] These are historically or culturally signified strata to the planetary population that have "seized" the universal for their own proprietary aims. It is in this way that the universal must be liberated from the factions that have brazenly done so.

Chapter 3

[20]   This is, after all here posited as the cultural class of upper-middle class liberal democrats—realizing all-too-well that universality is a socio-economic consideration that projects the social strata living purely in a "world of sense". As such they are individuals with a common purpose that never seems to constitute the universal to its most authentic conception. It is, as such, conceivable as an ideal then more as a reality.

[21]   What I here intend to posit here as "force" is something closer to dialectical or dialogical potencies, such that there is no individual in violation of the ethical standardization of the universality of genus as one that may only accommodate those for whom despicable acts of deception and legerdemain are never to be tolerated, posing a problem for both the conception of universality as of nature.

[22]   The idea that a phenomenology of the Self might be constituted through the realization of an "Other to abstraction", proposes something synthetic to the Self in consideration of the actuality of Self as posited upon a "field" or horizon of meaning. The notion that the correspondence of the Other to the Self as itself would be ontologically differentiated to representation is unclear, yet with these conditions it is such that the universality of genus be "perfectly" constituted intersubjectively, and that there are no synthetic actualities prior to the currency of contemplative acts, as such.

[23]   The conception that two self-identical universalities may be sustained in dialectical correspondence as subsumed to the particular is less tenable, positing an actuality that the objective Self represents itself upon coordinates in reality, rather than contingent structures fashioned by an overstimulated mind.

[24]   I will make it clear that the conception of "transcendental" here is where such things as are "producible" or "real" may also be "spiritual" *and* real. I am positing a transcendental relation as a real relation that has historical and cultural (political or economic) ties to the Self within its own reproducible symbolic imagination.

[25]   As such a reality only to the believer, which does not rule out the real world, as certain religious practices take into account the relationship between "God" and the world within a fully ontologically constituted object in reality, i.e. Christianity, Judaism, Islam, etc. It has been for centuries however, philosophy's task to eliminate the ontological proof of the existence of "God" as Kant would have it.

26   Such that "objective reality" is an object containing a form of knowledge to actuality, rather than the totality of all known things i.e., the reality of the object.
27   Inasmuch as particularizations may be universalized into a natural structuration to the biosphere, it is presupposed that agents of social transformation are particular to a binding set of propositions that posit a horizon of universal correspondence, thus.

Chapter 4

28   Of course, the objective natural Self propositionally coheres to the universality of genus, ergo the conception of reality to the "natural self" is something existing in relation to things such as they are identifiable as "universals", here posited as constitutive totalities singular to the wholeness of things, justly in distribution, though not in redistribution of properties natural to human organisms. As such, nature governing laws are these which are reflexive causes to the manner by which Being is universal and identical to itself in nature, both in content as in form.
29   Again, we are naturally identical to the Self in ego as in Being.
30   Inasmuch as contingencies may be unconscious, they also may be in self-positing dialectical correspondence as opposing authenticities—good versus evil, such as the case may be.
31   In other words, "commercial" mass-enterprise, is a project that may diffuse the energeia of ethical transformation to humanity as the state of transcendental nature.
32   The unconditioned is as though the order of a "world nature", or rather, a "nature world" that constitutes primordial being in essence, just as it does the conception of the Self as substance or ego i.e., natural and transcendental (transcendental in nature).
33   As such I posit industry culture as a phenomenon that exists in quantum reality to the "non-believers".
34   Such that preservation of a naturalization of the transcendental ego is still bound by ethical considerations that have not been challenged by an opposing faction also purporting to be in legislation of the universal thus, it is quite conceivable that there continue to exist particular hegemonic strata to the more authentic universalist agenda.
35   That the individuated Self is in ontological pre-possession of objects to the Self is more a question of where the immediacy of the universality of genus is presupposed—a given. As such, all natural Beings, and beings of transcendental nature have natural (world) objects posited within the Being of Self.
36   It is in this manner that an object of the nature-self becomes natural once it has been re-posited by the authentication to Being that has occurred through the universalization of the transcendental into its universal genus.

[37] Given that humanization would constitute the ethical transformation of the nature-self never in grid-lock with oppressive powers of observation, there is a "humanicization" to modal relations where the prevailing Self is the more ethically natural.

[38] As contingent actualities to nature, these regional, national and global institutions historically lay claim to universality as their own (as in Hegel). However, for the purposes herewith we identify universality as only conditionally embodied by the classification of subjects that are identical to themselves in their own natures.

[39] I am positing technology as part of evolutionary praxis in order to identify the merge between the natural environment, and the digital space intersecting with natural human substance.

[40] Yet a difficult proposition for the planet—a planetary universality that is able to order the natural world from a horizon of actuality that is purposive to the citizenry as the undivided reality of the future.

[41] Such as it is, the technological revolution has not enhanced humanity's natural evolutionary development so much as changed its trajectory. We were on the path of destruction to our own universal natural existence, and the time is now to become of the propositions in restoration of the impetus to authenticate the reality of evolutionary praxis to the point where its horizon of actuality is biased toward a universalization of the eradication of inauthenticities jeopardizing intentional judgments toward the realization of that end.

Afterword

At a horizon of the dawning of an age where humanity's truth is less than its universal conception, the search for a dimension to reality providing more than what it had our predecessors has become causal to the events that this planet is facing—given that the responsibilities for outcomes are never distributed in equalization to the notion that lives are more precious than the disasters that have resulted in direct consequences of the mass-pollution and exhaustion of life's primary natural resources. If it were that the questions had become societal ones—those identifying reason as the sole proprietary aim of organized ritualistic normative nation-states—we were better-off before they had condemned existence itself to an unbridled resurrection of obsolete manufactures of stability, propelling authenticity to a purposive darkness, only lit by the infernos ravaging the environment that had provided the very economic system it had enabled with a sentence to Hades, banishing knowledge from its space of restoration to organic unity from its inception in destructive powers, led by an avarice of reasonable conceptions unidentifiable as scientific facts. Funded by the watchdogs of economic necessity and personalized attempts to nullify the provisions of those that have fallen sway to a disappearance into the backwoods of Canadian monoculturalism[1]—creatures without possession of a popular edification of drives to the hopeful desires of those in seizure of the belonging of a particular class of unaccommodated residents—rights have been voided in protection of the contradictions that have been derived from unvetted laws, constituted by their acceptance of a trust that has been administrated through the prohibitions upon inalienable provisions to the former. We are, as such passengers upon a vessel that has set adrift less of its souls than previous world calamities, well within reach of any active contemplation, but more of its citizens than the previous three decades had; and for this reason the purposes of scientific progress must open the world to an objectivity that is not an either/or dynamic of an absolute acceptance of scientific judgment, or utter denial of a palatable constellation of speculative principles in concretion of the material evidence that we have with respect to a pernicious slew of planetary phenomena that feel as though divine providence has struck down the populations of Earth because of its 21st Century obsessions with objects of acquisition and desire.[2] We begin to reason that human undertaking exists, only as a possibility for those for whom justification has never before seen more relevance than what is acceptable to a public wanting nothing less than the chance to potentially squander the ethical spirit of the future, as though it were in an everlasting vicious circle of an iteration of the mistakes that had only emancipated what might be reified by an economic machinery leading to a breakdown of the body politic into stratified aberrations to a discourse becoming of the transmissible lunacy that had driven away the sensibilities of an entire generation—as though their contributions offered only a preamble to a regime that has no leaders—but only representatives to the capital that delivers us from its own destruction (turning the latter upon the environmental concerns). While catastrophizing into the night, without an experience of the world as a place that is globally ordered—and thereto approaching a diverse unit of connected possibilities existing as realities— the most isolated and self-contained communities have left behind the conception of universal planetary events, acting in unmediated cohesion to the actions of the state with only the enforcement of its inventory of indispensable laws within its authorities as an elected regulative body; having no uncertain terms, continuing to author the very contradictions of its structural envelopes to our architectural nature, toward an obfuscation of what could have illumined the sensible world with a meaning that were more than the complete abandonment of constitutive logic that were not indefatigably entwined with compromises underpinning a relapse to the past.[3] This is a take-no-prisoners approach, succumbing to a stultification of biopolitical engineering and acquisition of a truth to a reality that has yet to set foot upon the terrain of regions where success is more a measure of the potency to the win than the tenability to the propositions themselves—taken at face value and accepted as absolute pronouncements, distributing freedom only to those that have already become acquainted with the reality of their own losses—necessitating obedience and compliance to a system that has, in part, left behind constitutional provisions for a distribution of rights under governance closer to the totality of its own fortunes than those gifted the suffrage of historical positions in places where meaningful enterprise is a commodity only affordable to a class of the citizenry having yet to accept collective responsibility for an outcome perpetrated by its own monetization of its conception of humanity. This has never been delivered from the reality of its own most authenticated representations, or acknowledged as the image of what should perpetuate the purposes of human beings toward a horizon of progress that is more than the representations themselves—yet has not altogether abandoned the universal conception of our natures for a meaning that is too changeable in-itself to be rewarded with its own abstractions, as the progression from purpose into developmental progress; and a reasonable furtherance to the ideals of a reality that has been presented as factually identifiable to a world that perceived its truth as something that is undeniably as fit for consumption as its realization in the ethical understanding.

Within the latter, it is that factual evidence presides over the judgments themselves, but also that the conditions of judgment are particular to the universal conception of what has taken place—the event is one that is witnessed in tandem with a visual representation and the psychophysical pairing, identifiable as the localization of the specific action that has transpired. As such, an act of negligence or assault resulting in emotional or psychological trauma may be experienced sympathetically by an observer as a sensation given by its ontical characteristics, acting as a form of verifiability to the claim that is at stake in conception of a particular person, position or act that one has within the scope of an episteme that is symbolically entwined with transcendental realism—far from the ideal state-of-affairs for any given circumstance.[4] Nonetheless, the secrets that societies have possessed for many generations, without juridical repercussions, are many as they are few; as the silence of those disguised by their own fears of the reprisal of the accused are likely to wish that their silence had never been broken, thus. It is, as such, that the coordinates of the mistake that has been made has amplified the search for rationality, once the path of least resistance has also been broken by those that have found reprieve within their own conceptions of what constitutes innocence—an indemnification from the consequences that any such convictions would precipitate.[5] The laws of humanity outweigh the latter's conceptions of justice where concerns the subjective notion of the rights awarded those that replace the right with the wrong, given that their conception provides a skewed perception of what constitutes love or hate, the good or the bad—acting in accordance with one's position of trust, as though the life of each living being were not equally as important to their own when given the choice to perform an action, in promulgation of the virtues bestowed upon us all by our own *sense* of right and wrong. In centuries past, the question of what made human progress something edificial to the promotion of our lasting enterprise as the progenitors of purposive meaning, evolutionary development, scientific discovery and invention, resides upon the threshold of a pursuit of this that classed the unattainable with the readily available—providing accessibility to resources—both human and natural. It is upon each one of us to posit that the eviction of our souls from what constitutes the virtues of humans, is the landscape of what is condemnable to objective necessity, as an existence that must be considered an unfathomable one that had been universalized into the community substance, revealing a widespread series of conditions masking justice beyond the conception of the particular being, in search for a solution to what had transpired as the reality of a relationship that stands the chance of being replaced by the very consequences of the acts constituting punitive justification—without the notion that one would posit that a malicious act had taken place—but that violation had in fact transpired and action must be taken to resolve what had occurred in the most efficacious manner possible.[6] We must never turn a blind eye to the perceptual conditions of the symbolic dimension and its filiation with revelatory events, becoming experiences opening the mind to events that are well within purview.[7] Through the totality of existential occurrences available to the public forum of ontological presentability, the ramifications of an expository display of private activities initiates the possibility of a necessary cause of action, as here the subject may be considered complicitous, having avoided signs that something has happened that is not right and must be remedied, despite the consequences of having made allegations—perceived as someone bearing false witness in order to continue being accommodated by the comforts of the virtues continuously cast aside by those in possession of a different set of priorities more viable to the market economy. Against all odds, the latter must be converted into a space where virtue is not only an invisible commodity to be sold to the highest bidder, but something that will never be bargained-off as the way of life of a class of citizenry that is at odds with the universality of its very conception. We have never been a species that has succeeded throughout centuries untouched by the effects of our own choices, having yet to develop planetary existence to a plateau of truth that is not proprietary either to imposters or political renegades.[8] It is, as such, that humans would wish to depose one another time and time again, and someone having more of something than we do, becomes the target for our attentions; and thus the object of the game becomes to employ ourselves as the progenitors of justification seeking truth—philosophers having yet to merit the title but faced with the conditions whereby the ways of the former must perform their duties in order to remain viable in the business of philosophy. There is no ethical way by which a person should close their senses to what is happening, as this seems in the very nature of reason itself—to understand, to see, and to know. Why do we consequently shatter in the wake of our own responsibilities in denial of the reality that we would wish to be different than the one we experience? Is it that reality has condemned itself to the sense of choosing as more a matter of convenience than of discomfort, should the choice bring more harm to others from their own perspective? The problems of humanity are sometimes a function of actions taken by perceived duties, only resulting in disasters hurting great numbers of people; while the simplicity of avoidance is one where the "dirty little secret" is tucked away in a drawer until decades further down the line, and groups of individuals would have been punished for their actions—the effects of which will still have made the same impact upon the vulnerable and innocent. It is in this way that the choice is a difficult one—marked by more indecision than resolve— given that authentic acts of virtue in such cases offer no pleasure to the virtuous, only pain. With this, the question must be for the coward, how tolerant must I be of pain? The sensitive, as Hegel puts it best, have no place in philosophy—whereas Nietzsche assured us that compassion is only for fools. That we might further resolve the issue through discourse, while altogether avoiding debate, material evidence on top of what is self-evident to thinkers in possession of what is standardized within close-nit community relations as the "ones in the know"—never to be confused with the suspiciously paranoid interlopers, thinking that their participation is required or even desired—necessitating professionals of alethic modalities and deontic normativity, resisting the old-fashioned ways of societal miscreants acting in caprice upon their own antiquated traditions of Draconian ritual sacrifice, to be left out of the spectrum of thought associated with these types of judgment; lest the very conception of the latter becomes tainted by a protectorate of the same body politic being condemned by the ones truly responsible for the very actions that have taken place, for whom the destruction of life would lead to more pain than is acceptable to the authenticity of the virtues associated with the universal conception of the transparency of choice in filiation with evolutionary justice.[9] This provided, the pursuit of a universal conception of justice is an order that has evaded humanity for the duration of the time we have had upon this Earth. How is one to accept responsibility for cause of action, when the precipitation of effects exposes the objectivity of Being to suspicions of foul play or nefarious intent—an inversion of the allegations the community is willing to hide—that their secrets are for the purposes of protecting whom they prefer in more ways than one? Someone who is seen to be virtuous in every way imaginable to narrow-minded conceptions of universality has only been legislated by ne'er-do-wells and naysayers. Those that follow their ambitions with consistency to a conformity—with benefactors ranging from serial rapists to run-of-the-mill sex offenders—those guilty of criminal negligence, white-collar criminals, and institutional maniacs, to name of few. I know full-well that the light shines upon the accuser, more than it does the accused under any such circumstances as are these; it is only that the crucible of the desires of the most favoured are the same as those of the victors of a universality that is recognized only by the narrow intellects encompassing its collective articulation—perpetuating the conditions of the same authorized sense of belonging—prone to despoil the purposes of authenticity with a compliance to the cultural machinery of imbeciles and haphazardly obsequious conformists.

Alas, it is thus that the most anointed sense of resplendence supplying nature with the form by which the laws of humanity are to be consigned to those offering the possibility of safety that there is nothing standing before expressions of self within justifications universal in ethical conception, and the acknowledgements to the reality of the people as the truth of spirit, identifiable as the wholeness and completeness of the rights retained therein—the restoration of what has been resourcefully exchanged in the passage of time, from our inception as a species, to the very positions that we have taken upon this planet as survivors of the multitude of natural disasters occupying Earth—the soul of the becoming of an age where we will either bestow upon the future the becoming of a horizon that is absolute to progress, or relative to modal relations in the transformation of society to a place where it is conformable only to the laws of reason that may be constituted by nature's governing laws, thus. That the protectorate of the dream is a transpositional stance in a residuum of phenomenological actualities, particular to the universality of transparency, is an awakening to a trust that the expository givens of our proprietary extensions of being exist—residing within the plenitude of a differentially unbridled aim to resound upon the world stage with an everlasting self-realization that is objectivated to itself as the evolutionary becoming of a developmental causality to the projection beyond the threshold of the lived experience that is phonemically represented to the pre-reflexive cogito—from which the purposes of this existence become perfections in the doing of what propels us onward the furtherance of a humanity that is symbolized through its own archeological techne. We reside well within the auspices of a species with the cause to effectuate a bioeconomic revolution that will transport the meaning of our time to the nouveau of a perpetuation that condemns fallibility in judgment less than it does the exposition of planetary ethical transformability, to where it exists as the natural horizon of our most fathomable aspirations that have been developed through acceptance of the universal teleology of developmental aims themselves—the spirits of history are never these which only arrive upon the precipice of the nullification of an authenticity that has transcended its origins in modernism, only to steal away into the night as the reality of the age in which meaning has not become the economic exchange resolving to author human relations as an expendable commodity, perceiving justice as the mediating force toward acquisition of the former. In this sense, the purposes of humanity are never lost to despots or madmen that have denied the sensible understanding, never identifiably within reason—the experience of truth that has driven speculative conclusions and practical intentions toward what constitutes a changeability to the material purposes of justifiability as dialectical, and never simply this which is conclusive upon its own resourced circumspective suspicions. It is with the former that the evolutionary nature of the socio-natural world will enter the nature-self, as its transmutable exchange toward a becoming that is the transformation of its usefulness as an object to humanity that is natural in its own transcendentality and transcendental in its own nature—of a transposition to the horizon of an actuality that has been dawning upon the planet since the appearance of primordial beings—now projecting toward a future that is within the vision of the possibility of its conditional state of fluxion, into an authenticity that has never been lost to the earthly confines that gifted it with life; but will also never become anything more than a period in the planet's history where genus of a species were unable to resolve its differential calculus as a fallible creature, and were ultimately doomed to perish just as other species had. We are more than this, and must find the path toward the horizon of what is natural to the causes propelling the species beyond its disintegration into a self-destructive race that has yet to realize the reality set forth by the effects of what cries for the necessity of change, and the realization of a potential that is within our grasp—yet consistently slips way into the night as though the purposes of our time have never been less aware of the universality symbolizing the reality of our collective aims.

The historical accord we have with our past is precisely the identification of conditions where pathways of the future may be redrawn. This is the moment where what is chosen as the universal reality of global societies will begin to plot a course at the planetary scale—individual family units, municipal communities, regional zones, nation-states, and the world itself are reflexively entwined with one another as to the choices defining the direction the former take from the perspective of those with accessible services to infrastructure, administrable at local and global levels. Each of the former act in correspondence with the latter two categories in various ways, i.e., municipal communities may hold world events, just as the world may also be paying particular attention to the dynamics that make municipal news worthy, i.e. Jerusalem, and in this sense in both cases there is an intersection between the conception of the village or town such as it is, or the world such as it is *vis-à-vis* the town as in McLuhan's global village. Such as it is, the world *as* the town is something quite daunting where concerns individuals' liberties and conceptions of personal and professional freedoms during a *global* pandemic, while a town such as Washington, D.C., imposing its will upon global societies, would never be accepted by many of the countries that have only tolerated the U.S. where it did not intervene in its own affairs. While, as political theorists are well-aware, America has always considered itself the model society, transferring its culture to other parts of the world, just as other developed nation-states have throughout history.[10] However, as history has shown, liberty is removed from existence when a society believes that it represents its very conception, attempting to transform other societies in such a manner as to force them to live in a world designed by them, and not in accordance with its own customs and conceptions of what is normative from the historical perspective. Yet the vision for a market driven, labelled, inclusive multicultural society prioritizing the structured freedoms of the Western World as a template for progress and resourced development, will never be accepted in many parts of the globe historically entwined with conceptions of the natural world as radically dissociated from Western cultural traditions, while the identification of rampant marginalization of racialized communities in North-America has been received by the public with a percentage of acrimony, continuing in denial of the historical landscape of our violent past in pursuit of the establishment of the "New World". But it's easy to discern that rhetoric offers politicians the skeleton key to winning an election—what is accomplished while in power is an altogether unknowable series of conditions. What we do know, is what has happened in the United States during the Trump presidency has made their politics subject to global ridicule, with many opposing powers like China and Russia turning up their noses to the very thought of the superiority of the West. I, for one, would proudly call myself Canadian more than ever before if I perceived the road to reconciliation with First Nations in concretion; and the universality of Canada a possibility that were attainable in decades to come. Since the advent of universal health care, there is a compulsory advantage to making universality a societal reality, through the resolution of the differences that still make laws something inaccessible to the preservation of the universal conception of justice. Were we to see less crime, homelessness, destructive patterns of addiction, misguided mental health concerns that were lost to the system, and a total and complete elimination of poverty with the object to continue developing research protocols in order to discover cures to life-threatening illnesses, the country will have established the correct priorities for the future. With this, there is also the move toward protection of the environment, by putting an end to excessive use of fossil fuels, deforestation, and contamination of the water supply.[11] We must also continue to protect wildlife and develop new systems of waste renewability by using science to discover progressive ways to make our disposables reusables for energy. The ethics of sending disposable waste out into space is a contentious one, since this would potentially damage the trajectory of our planet toward its carbon emission goals. As any physicist might tell you, it's not a good idea to have planetary waste just burn up in the sun's heat with orbital concerns becoming more part of the discourse surrounding climate change—some of which have been entertained by prominent scientists. In my lifetime it always seemed a far-fetched proposition we would ever surpass our *friends* to the South as the carriers of any such notions—those suggesting we send our disposables into the sun to rid ourselves of it.[12] This would be the equivalent of loading up the furnace with household garbage and still expecting to have a household free from poisonous emissions, would it not? Well, what say you physicists? Is it feasible that we could just incinerate our trash upon the sun? For it is that all matter in the universe never ceases to be matter, but only undergoes change. In this sense, changeable matter is what presupposes the notion of changeable existence, and changeable existence presupposes the notion of changeable matter. Now as the existence of matter necessarily presupposes experience, it is that existence presupposes matter itself. In this sense all things that have material form possess existence. It is not that all matter is a living thing, but that matter itself presupposes that something exists and therefore where there is matter, there is life. In this way, matter is the precondition for the existence of life, and life is the precondition for the experience of matter. Such as it is, anywhere in the Solar System where there is matter presupposing the existence of life, it is that this is impossible given that the experience of life presupposes the existence of matter, and as there is no living thing that presupposes the existence of matter where there is only matter and no life—then the experience of matter does not presuppose the existence of life. As such the changeable matter of disposable human waste presupposes the existence of life, but life does not presuppose the existence of changeable human matter, as the interventions that may be undertaken by living things may halt the changeability of matter. In this sense, human disposable waste on the planet may be changed in such a way as to propose life through the progression from changeable waste to changeable matter; and in this way, it is that the matter, so changed, may only continue to exist in the universe insofar as it has changed in material form, i.e., solid, liquid, gas, to something only existing at the quantum level, as particles that pose no threat to the astronomical centrifuge of orbital trajectories. For we have reached the precipice of a critical mass with the planet ablaze and careful considerations are in order to resume the pursuit of a sustainable outcome for humanity. There is a breadth and a scope to the means by which this may be achieved, and how governments and individual societies may act in response to the disasters facing the planet—offering a clue as to how we must further proceed.

With the discourse at hand, one is readily swayed from the Self as subject, since considerations that are ontological ones are identifiable as these which deal with beings, how they are represented, and how they relate to the objects that accompany the sensible experiences of the natural environment that embodies us, and that we ultimately embody. But that cosmogenic considerations concern us with universal substance—as all things in the universe in possession of identifiable or measurable properties—the conception of the qualities inherent humanity are never cast aside elucidations belonging to questions with respect to the nature of self, or of the self as a substance that is inextricably entwined with the universe *in toto*. While continuing to identify most of us as planetary subjects, in due course, it will become necessary to concern ourselves with how the behaviour of humankind will be affected by things such as space travel and extended periods of time in closed quarters with unlike people— quite topical to most science fiction in the notion that there will be unresolvable conflicts that could jeopardize projects, and the character vetting process to identify questionable subjects will have to be exceedingly rigorous. As we have yet to resolve most of the conflicts affecting Earth's progress as a space where the proposed unity of humanity is currently beyond our grasp, it seems that the only place it may be feasible is in the stars—the world's horizon as it is from the perceptual actuality of the age in which we now live has not yet transformed toward the absolute goal of a future where war is an obsolete and costly business that humanity no longer has the resiliency with which to engage. In fact, that it still exists as an option, shines a dull and incompatible light upon the horizons of the real world experience that any universe such as ours, and *theirs*, would have the colossal gall to withstand, in consideration of the vicissitudes of what is condemnable the spaces of representation that we have within modal relations; just as it does the pre-reflexive cogito that allows a being to pursue aims that make any such conceptions of reality feasible. Insofar as the rationality of humanity has never been lost to unfathomable conclusions that have seeded an ineffable trail of infinite impossibilities, the means by which things realized are to become known are fundamental to the causes that project the manufacture of the resourced energeia that is ours to consume where it is universal to existence on Earth; but only provisional insofar as the experiences of human beings are particular to the involvement that subjects have within their own individuated lives— providing a course has been set for the most ethical expression of what is to become more than simply an idyllic conception of what is transcendental to the material goods posited by the natural world. If for a moment we were to expose the understanding to a vision of the future possessing no functionary structuration, and it were identified as the purpose of humanity to fulfill the proposition because of some perceived authenticity to the latter, we would have surely delivered ourselves from collective survival into a torrent of objections from the universe itself—that the habitat of our planet would be so bold as to send its troubles into the heavens as recourse to the fallibility of the conclusions that had been so deliberately authored by previous generations.

With explorations of this nature in the plans for the future, the question as to what constitutes ethical endeavor comes to the fore of the present discourse, since we will, after all, be making sacrifices to the global efforts to slow climate change—though as of 2021 C.E., it seems that the planet has revolted against generations of industrial development full-throttle, and it would be naïve to imagine the problem simply disappearing any time in the foreseeable future. We are presented with a horizon where the planet is being destroyed by the environment's response to the industrial economic priorities offering a greater degree of convenience to the population of the developed world, with an outcome profiting irrefutable evidence that the industrial revolution's economic structure has irreparably harmed Earth, and we must concentrate more planetary resources toward the gradual restoration of what is left of this precious planet. The science required to assist in this process has not yet progressed to the point where the proposition of an immediate course of action is self-evident. Alongside this, the behaviour of seventy to eighty percent of the developed world would have to be drastically changed, such that the restoration process may be undertaken as a universal ethical imperative.[13] Holding summits and positioning targets within the Paris Accord has not yet initiated a global manifestation of the collective will to abide within those targets, as the population continues to prioritize the restoration of its freedoms, especially now that the vaccine targets for the global pandemic Covid-19 have nearly been met throughout many of the developed countries, but not across the board—on a planetary level. The universality of the acceptance that the world was facing a global pandemic as posited by WHO (World Health Organization) was not universally accepted, with many individuals resisting the restrictions upon their lives; creating economic hardship, destroying relationships, elevating levels of domestic abuse and suicide, exacerbating pre-existing mental-health conditions while creating new mental-health problems for some—altogether compounded with floods, wildfires, and intolerable heat waves causing sudden death coming to pass. Without even turning on the television, anyone on the planet with or without a wireless device realizing something undeniably foreboding happening to the planet, reveals tribal communities, religious sects, and esoteric mystics perceiving the spiritual retaliation of the supervenience of gods, God, or a Necromancer. Educated minds must also recognize the correspondence that humanity has with nature and the natural world; and for this purpose we must accept that our collective health universally depends upon the amelioration of our habitat—throughout the age of modernity conceived as civilization or civil society, but always only insofar as it were acting in correspondence with Nature. At what point will *we* fully come to respect the natural environment that must not simply serve the purposes of our consumption and avarice, but must also be conserved to preserve the health of the planet, and also ourselves? Modern science has delivered many advancements to the way in which we live, with elongated lifespan, treatments for many illnesses that were once life-threatening, and a higher standard of living for more people than previous generations. But still the ravages of poverty and disease dominate portions of Earth, and we are far from creating the perfect world that so many renown philosophers of oddity seem to think had somehow materialized for the better only a few years prior to now. It seems the Chicken Littles of the world were for the most part entirely ignored—condemned to lunatic asylums or prisons out of desperation, while the wealthy prophesied something in the way of Nostradamus. Knowledge—the most valuable commodity, second only to time, it seems, is consistently utilized to further evolving sciences like GMOs (Genetically Modified Organisms), and the effort to bring technology and nature together is still part of ad hoc industries, now in the early stages of the effort to position humanity on a path toward an equalization of the food supply, while many know how controversial these types of interventions are to naturalists—many ethical considerations involving genetic engineering propose that such scientific interventions of nature are harmful—both to animals and humans, and may negatively impact the disadvantaged populations of the globe. Without resourcing the full scope of economic intervention as a medium toward a horizon of a healthier planet, a horizon of renewable green energy only necessitates economic intervention to the degree that it does not mandate an expansion of an already imploding global economy. More growth amounts to less equality, more disease, and fewer opportunities to resolve the present conditions jeopardizing the well-being of humanity at the planetary level. Should we in the West come out on top, that does not mean that the problems of the world will not continue to find us time and time again, just as they always have. This position has always been the attitude that the developed world had taken, but it is that the miracle that needs to happen is no such miracle, but quite a practical implement of an infrastructural universalization of the renewable sources of energy available, and a developmental adjustment to the economic priorities of global industries toward a model echoing this of a fragmented and once overstimulated population, one offering a progressive humanism where the nature of being is to see beyond the machine and perceive what it is of and for existence—to create more than is possible through economic drives alone—resolving to an evolutionary development of the discovery of ourselves, as able to function without the expansion of our needs in order to outmode the competition inherent of the capitalist agenda. The pathway toward this horizon is one that has been jeopardized by a virtual incineration of the necessary conditions of progress, such that the landscape of the actualities of our time identifies the interpretation of reason to be based upon norms that have been implemented by the structural edification of a system that is already broken. The changes that we must undergo belong to the purposes of the age in which we universally occupy spaces upon planet Earth, yet the occupation of Earth is not of a universality that articulates the becoming of the historical necessities of the past—positing a naturalization of the existence that we have as total to the experience of the Self as integral to the choices that are made *vis-à-vis* conditions generative of institutional avoidance; where the meaning of our purpose must be to do what is within our collective means—with the impetus to devote our natural Self to the preservation of the conditions evolving the qualitative existence of humanity beyond its transitional phase, toward the horizon of an actuality that is revolutionary in its appeal to the laws of humanity as universally identical to authentic being; and transformational insofar as they are particular to the restoration of the environmental conditions predicated upon the actions that we take, and the choices representative of the causes that will come to decide the outcome for the totality of human endeavor for the generations to follow.

Notes

¹ A refutation of multiculturalism is not what is here intended—it is rather to consider the matter of biodiversity in its ontological difficulty concerning the sustainable forms by which ontical properties may not possess possible co-existence that would unify the conditions of representable existence in such a manner as to allow for a horizon of reality that offers an expression of life as a uniform terrain, without contradictory dialectical elements that may jeopardize humanity's inexorable pursuit of evolutionary undertaking and fathomable reproducible systems integral to the progress that will map the planetary trajectory for the centuries ahead.

² Provided human consumption does not destroy the possibilities for a revolution of authenticity in progress is posited as necessary to survival, rather than its stultification in objects identified as necessities toward the realization of happiness—time will most certainly consume us more with the deterioration of what is constitutive to the developmental infrastructures that will offer a more refined existence to a greater percentage of the global population with the transfer of a renewable platform of reusable planetary objects.

³ The past of which is widely known as one of the darker periods in the history of Western culture (2001-2020). As a culture that were authored less by its own leaders than the leaders by it, approaching their political agendas as a measure of the prescription of popular demand over a progressive authentication of resolutions that would lead to a possible disassembly of the North-American populous into unstratified disintegrating masses overstimulated by the dialectical contradictions endemic of the American way of life, as such.

⁴ Such as it is, the experience of certain mental conditions or psychical states that are experienced from a clinical position by a health professional, are also experienced by a vulnerable member of the public as the delusional context of their own personal traumas or problems with the Western standardization of assimilation into communities, society, and industrialized institutions or places of employment, worship, recreation and enjoyment, etc.

⁵ Such as it is the indemnity of the trusted support systems of the modern age are yet to become exposed to the realities of the truths that have led certain individuals to pursue the conclusion of their lives without discovering the certainties available through more transparent networks and support systems in pursuit of the common goal of justice.

[6] With the eventuality of possible social transformation upon the horizon, the conception of any such thing as the reality of justice will not be as unfathomable as it has once seemed.

[7] Though as Lacan had posited in *Écrits, Éditions De Seuil, 1966.*, the symbolic representation may only constitute reality where posited in liaison with the totality of the world in context of the experience as perceived, in order to rule out the images' potential delusive context. However, there are certain logical exceptional conditions where the relative authenticity of a symbolization is representative of a factual occurrence that is grounded upon *a posteriori* judgments, by which justificatory evidence has been revealed.

[8] As such, it has always been that it is the culture of the connected and the elite projecting a dialectical suffusion as those with possessory rights within their factions, only to extend their positions toward their opponents insofar as unreasonable limitations are imposed continuously upon the social strains in pursuit of an emancipatory justification of their own provisional self-valuation.

[9] The conception of "evolutionary justice" is here marked as the condition whereupon the systems of attainable representative functionality are extended to horizons integral of the ideas that sustain transmissible forms of human energy, such that it may become renewable to the enterprise of developmental reforms to the sources of life that determine a more favourable outcome that endeavors to constitute a universalization of "the safety zone".

[10] As such the history of colonization of underdeveloped countries has been rampantly identified as the root cause of most of the civil unrest that has occurred for several centuries; it is more a matter of transcending the past as a movement that sustains in developmental contributions and abandoning the conditions imposed by this which structures impossible conditions to the restoration of an authentic landscape of multiform expressions of the viability to nature—not as a resource, but as the environment where universal claims may be reasonably made.

[11] This will of course take many decades to achieve within reason, as the form by which such goals are attained may condition certain individuals in such a manner as to purpose conformity to the universal legislation of what will allow for the transformation toward a more sustainable global environment.

[12] This is of course intended in mere conjecture as a possible intervention, toward the possibility of a saturation of the global environment by disposable human waste—we are producing more unviable waste than any previous historical societies have—by way of

overconsumption, overstimulation to the economy, and *overpopulation.*

[13] With the global population not yet instituted in such a manner so as to formalize coalescence between every nation-state, the invocation of a planetary uniformity—at least in conception of beneficial aims that are universally understood as particular to the identification of uniform conditions posited through the localization of transformative initiatives—may be implemented by more progressive states in pursuit of the "brass ring", that will ultimately determine a position of domination for one regional assembly that performs any such transformative capacitation—through the forms by which universalizable goals may be officiated through administrable conditions shaped in application of the eventual transition toward a bioeconomic restoration of the authenticity to the positions determinable of a restoration to the evolutionary development of humanity's conditional sustainability (i.e. progressive evolutionary governments that prioritize natural progress alongside gene mapping and ethical bioengineering).

INDEX

Acknowledgments

This book, brief as it may be, is the culmination of an entire generation's worth of reflection, and I consider myself fortunate to have been able to compose it, continuing in the search for more answers. I am grateful to have been given another chance to express my ideas on such matters, though I sense a depth of responsibility that I am not entirely certain I am willing to accommodate. My studies have led me toward a picture of the world as I would wish it to become, rather than what it is, and I am purposive toward the completion of a much wider scope in the field that I have chosen to pursue. The circumstances that have led me here have been agonizingly difficult at times, as I am pushing for a more complete image of what constitutes the reality of this age, the reality of the Self, and the horizon of possibility that has fallen into darkness in recent years. However, where there is still light, is precisely the place that I have found fellowship and belonging, and that place is the field of philosophy. I have been pursuing the discipline on my own for twenty-five years, and it has led me to certain extremes that have contributed to both the arts and the sciences, and I have enjoyed positing a vision for humanity that constitutes the world as it could someday become if we continued to apply excellence in judgment as in choice. When I departed Vancouver in 2001, I discovered the meaning of the word *autonomy* and chose to throw myself into practicing and studying. The first professional philosopher I encountered was James R. Muir (University of Winnipeg)—strangely sitting in on a lecture after the September 11 attacks. Fortunately the lecture was on Alan Bloom's *The Closing of the American Mind* and his translation of Plato's *Republic*. Shortly thereafter, I attended a conference with philosopher Sir John Ralston Saul at the Fort Garry Hotel and realized that the questions that I had were not as comprehensible as I had formerly believed. The following year I had already fully imported the concept of the transcendental into my mind, yet perceived what I was experiencing as perfectly real and truthful; and to be followed rather than denied. However, as it turns out what I received was the best of both possible worlds—a transcendentality that is coherent to reality, and a reality that is coherent to transcendental symbolization and the social imaginary. It was not without some digging deep into the recesses of my mind for conclusive answers to my questions that I have finally come closer to a solution, and remain a devoted follower of truth to this day. As my skepticism has always flourished in the wake of the metaphysical project that I have pursued as well as endured, the figures from Aristotle to Descartes, and from Descartes to postmodernism remain central to the area in cognitive research I wish to acknowledge. I wish to thank colleagues at academia.edu. Dr. Carl Matheson, Dr. Neil McArthur, Dr. Arthur Schafer (University of Manitoba), Dr. Kenneth R. Westphal, Dr. George Tomlinson, Dr. Michele Schmidt, Rob Hamilton, Bruce Hopkins, David Chisholm, Ed Henderson, and Marcelo Vieta (University of Toronto). I also wish to thank Dr. Ivan J. Kowalchuk and his assistant Heather for providing my Being with reasonable boundaries all these years—and most especially my Mother for allowing me to learn and grow well into my adult life—none of this would exist if not for her. I was also fortunate enough to have come from an intelligent family, with several gifted siblings pushing me to achieve more than they might realize; and with the passing of the family patriarch I will regard the challenges he proposed for life a generous source of inspiration for the difficulty in finding truth to the representations that one has—he made it as hard as can be, and I hope it was well worth it.